INSTANT POT® OBSESSION

INSTANT POT®
obsession

THE ULTIMATE
Electric Pressure Cooker Cookbook
for Cooking Everything Fast

JANET A. ZIMMERMAN

SONOMA
PRESS

To Dave, my soul mate and kitchen partner. And to Adeena, Paul, and Kate—wish you were here to see your little sister get published.

CONTENTS

INTRODUCTION

To say I'm obsessed with kitchen equipment is the understatement of the year; it's like saying Shakespeare wrote a couple of plays. My excuse is that I develop and write recipes for cookbooks and culinary classes, but the truth is my obsession started long ago, back when I worked in a cookware store. Acquaintances walking into our home kitchen are often dumbstruck when they see the wall of cookware: stainless steel and copper pots and pans, cast iron skillets, Dutch ovens, casserole and gratin dishes of all sizes. Then they turn and spy the wall of tools and appliances: mixers and food processors, spice grinders and mandolines, electric slicers, slow cookers, vacuum sealers, and sous vide circulators. (It's probably just as well that they don't know about the bakeware in the bedroom closet.)

Some kitchen passions prove to be mere infatuations that don't stand the test of time, but when I find a tool I like, I stick with it. I have two stovetop pressure cookers that I've been using for years, and I was perfectly happy with them. But I kept hearing murmurs about the Instant Pot®. Soon, friends in the food world weren't only talking about it, they were gushing. Finally, one made its way to my countertop. I admit, I felt vaguely guilty, as if I were cheating on trusted friends.

But the Instant Pot® has turned out to be more than a passing fancy. Not only does it pressure cook, but it can also function as a slow cooker, yogurt maker, and rice cooker. It's easy to use and about as hands-off as an appliance can be—just set it and walk away. Or (if you're like me) take some time to prep a few ingredients, set it and walk away, and then come back and do a little more work to finish a dish. Even when it doesn't save me much time, the fact that it doesn't require any attention can be just as helpful.

This incredibly popular electric pressure cooker fits into pretty much any cooking style, from quick and simple to time consuming and complex. It's great at one-pot meals but equally useful for preparing ingredients for future dinners—or breakfasts, lunches, snacks, and desserts.

Some home cooks use the appliance for a few tasks only, like tried-and-true soup or stew recipes, stocks and broths, or pot roast, all of which it excels at. But others have taken to it in a bigger way. These cooks wake up and think, "What can I make in my Instant Pot®?" They use it every day, all day long. It's changed their cooking habits so much that they find themselves wishing they had two. So they buy another.

No matter which of these groups you belong to, this book will make you the master of your Instant Pot®. If your use of it is limited to a couple of recipes, I will show you how much more it can do, and expand your repertoire to include cool, unexplored functions and tasty new dishes. If you already use it daily, I will provide you with tips and tricks to make it perform at its best (and possibly dispel some misconceptions), and help you prepare the best meals you've ever made.

Meanwhile, you'll find me trying to explain the situation to my stovetop pressure cookers. "Really, guys, I swear it's not you."

CHAPTER 1

A HEALTHY OBSESSION

Isn't it great when your obsessions turn out to be good for you? That's the case for those of us who are obsessed with the Instant Pot®. Even if you're not consciously trying to cook healthier meals, chances are excellent that it's been a good influence. For some beginning cooks, this special pressure cooker has inspired them to cook from scratch for the first time ever. And there's no doubt that cooking from scratch—using fresh ingredients and having control over what goes into your dinner—is a very healthy habit to form. For more experienced cooks, the time savings from cooking under pressure means that healthier meals are a possibility even on busy weeknights.

HOW MANY IS TOO MANY?

While an Instant Pot® can't cook everything, the range of things it can do keeps us plenty busy. Often, the most challenging limitation is having only one! You want to make yogurt, but that means the pot will be tied up for dinner. Or you're making a main dish in the pot, and while you have a great side dish recipe for the pot, the timing doesn't work to cook them simultaneously. Does this sound familiar?

Oh, sure, you can often figure out a way to work it out. The pot is great for braised dishes, which can be cooked ahead and reheated on the stove top while you're pressure cooking rice or mashed potatoes. But when you can't, you might find yourself wishing you had a second one. You're not alone. Many die-hard Instant Pot® enthusiasts have two—and some are even considering a third. Some want to upgrade, buying either a larger size or a newer version with more features.

Your Options

Currently, the Instant Pot® comes in three sizes (5 quarts, 6 quarts, and 8 quarts) and three models (LUX, DUO, and Smart).

LUX. Available in 5-quart and 6-quart sizes, this pot has six cooking functions: pressure cooker, sauté/browning, slow cooker, rice cooker, steamer, and warmer.

Those who initially purchased the LUX may find that they want the additional features or the bigger size of the newer models. That doesn't mean that the much-loved LUX isn't useful; it just depends on how your needs and interests change with continued use.

DUO. Available in 5-quart, 6-quart, and 8-quart sizes, this pot has all the same cooking functions as the LUX, plus the addition of a yogurt setting. It also has two pressure levels, low and high, rather than just one.

SMART. Available only in the 6-quart size, this is the newest model as of this writing. It is Bluetooth enabled, which means it can be programmed and monitored through a variety of apps for smartphones.

Do you need, or even want, more than one Instant Pot®? That depends on your cooking style, your kitchen space, the time you can dedicate to cooking, your budget, and your other kitchen appliances. If you have a slow cooker and you use it frequently, then it might take the place of a second pot. If you have another pressure cooker (stove top or electric), it might work as your backup pot. If not, a second Instant Pot® might be more tempting.

If you're seriously considering a second (or third) pot, make your choice wisely. If you have a LUX, it's well worth considering a DUO. Even if you think you'll never make yogurt, having two pressure levels is a big plus. If your family is expanding, then consider a larger size for your second pot. You can use that for main dishes and use the older, smaller one for side dishes or desserts. The possibilities are endless.

Keep in mind that most dishes that can be cooked in an Instant Pot® can be made with traditional cooking methods. So if you can't (yet) afford a second pot or don't have room for it, don't despair. You can still pull off the same delicious meals using a combination of cookware. And as anyone obsessed with the Instant Pot® likely already knows, at least a couple of times a year there are online sales that really crash the price of the appliance, which has helped many go from wanting to owning a second pot.

INSTANT POT® TERMINOLOGY

I don't use abbreviations in this book, but if you read websites or belong to online discussion groups dedicated to the Instant Pot®, you'll find that, like many groups, they seem to have their own language. Here are a few of the common terms and abbreviations you may see:

IP: Instant Pot®

NATURAL PRESSURE RELEASE (NPR OR NR): Letting the pressure inside the pot drop on its own

PC: Pressure cooker or pressure cooking

POT-IN-POT (PIP) COOKING: Cooking ingredients in a bowl or baking dish placed on a trivet inside the Instant Pot®

QUICK RELEASE (QR): Moving the pressure release valve to release the steam all at once

SLING: A strip of aluminum foil used to remove a bowl from the Instant Pot® (see page 16)

TRIVET: A metal or silicone rack (usually with handles) on which food is placed for steaming in the Instant Pot®

BEYOND THE BASICS

Even for veteran users, these handy appliances can hold some surprises. For instance, until I started thinking seriously about recipes for this cookbook, I had no idea I could make my favorite lemon curd in it. No more standing over the stove! Sure, you know it as a pressure cooker, slow cooker, rice cooker, and (possibly) yogurt maker. You might use it every day, or several times a day. But did you know about these functions?

PROOF BREAD DOUGH. Use the yogurt function or the slow cooker on low for the perfect temperature in which to let dough rise.

BAKE IN IT. Technically, you're steaming, so don't expect light, airy cakes or brown, crusty bread. But many quick breads and even yeast breads can be made in the Instant Pot®. Banana bread, anyone?

COOK FROZEN FOODS. Dinner plans sometimes change, and even the most organized among us can forget to take that chunk of meat out of the freezer, so it's nice to know that you can cook foods without thawing them first. I admit, I'm torn about this one, as it's undeniable that you'll lose something in texture and flavor if you cook frozen meats in your Instant Pot®. But, in other cases (shrimp, for instance), frozen is actually the best option.

PAMPER YOUR POT

While the Instant Pot® is a great tool on its own, you can expand its capabilities and make your cooking life even easier with a few well-chosen accessories. But before going wild and buying a ton of additional equipment, look through what you have already; chances are you can repurpose some items from your cupboards. If you want to buy accessories, consider checking out online Instant Pot® discussion groups. Their members can alert you to useful items and sale prices. Here are some extras you may find helpful:

EXTRA SEALING RING—OR TWO. Not only can silicone rings pick up various odors (see the FAQ on page 21 for advice on how to minimize this), but despite their durability, they can get stretched or nicked. And if your ring is compromised, you can't use your pot. These rings are available only through Instant Pot®.

PRESSURE IN THE POT: A REFRESHER

In the simplest terms, pressure cookers work because the boiling point of liquid depends on the atmospheric pressure.

Conventional Pressure Cooking

In a conventional pot, whether it's on the stove or in the oven, water-based cooking liquids will never get above 212°F (100°C). Water boils and turns to steam, and the steam dissipates, even if the pot has a lid. But in the sealed chamber of a pressure cooker, the water that turns to steam can't escape, which increases the pressure in the pot. With the higher pressure, more energy is necessary for the water to boil, so the temperature rises.

Instant Pot® Pressure Cooking

In this appliance, the low pressure is between 6 and 7 psi (pounds per square inch), with a temperature between 230°F and 233°F (110°C and 112°C). The high pressure is between 10.2 and 11.6 psi, with a temperature between 240°F and 245°F (115°C to 118°C). Once the pot comes to pressure, the liquid inside is *not* boiling. In most cases, that's part of the point of using a pressure cooker: You want hotter—but not boiling—liquid for braising, since boiling meat toughens it, or for stock making, since boiling clouds the stock. However, as the pressure reduces, either naturally or quickly through the steam vent, the still-hot liquid will begin to boil. *Always* exercise caution when removing the lid, since the liquid within may be boiling violently.

Finally, because cooking under pressure requires boiling liquid, it's important to make sure you have enough liquid. Since virtually no evaporation occurs once the lid is locked into place, you don't need a lot; generally, a cup or so is sufficient. And keep in mind that many foods give off liquid while cooking, so beginning with around a half cup may be fine, too.

LID THAT FITS THE INNER POT. This can be handy, especially if you plan to make yogurt or use the slow cooker function. If you have a lot of cookware, you may already have one that fits. If not, Instant Pot® sells glass lids specially made for the inner pot.

EXTRA INNER POT. Available only through Instant Pot®, these come in both stainless steel and—for the 6-quart DUO—nonstick-coated ceramic. The nonstick is very useful if you cook with milk, as milk proteins tend to stick when they cook. If you want to make yogurt, the nonstick version is ideal.

SMALL (6- TO 7-INCH) SPRINGFORM PAN OR DEEP CAKE PAN WITH A REMOVABLE BOTTOM. If you plan to make desserts such as cheesecakes, these are indispensable.

METAL OR CERAMIC 1- TO 1½-QUART BOWL. You'll want one of these for cooking "pot-in-pot" dishes such as quiches or stuffing.

COLLAPSIBLE STEAMER BASKET. While the Instant Pot® comes with a steaming trivet, you'll be able to fit a lot more food in a full-size steamer basket. Make sure it has a short or collapsible handle so it fits in the pot.

SILICONE STEAMING TRIVET. Not only can you use this for steaming foods like fish fillets, but its handles allow you to remove baking dishes from the pot instead of using a foil sling.

TALL (2- TO 3-INCH) TRIVET. While this isn't necessary, it can be handy if you want to cook in layers.

Other useful kitchen tools that you probably already have include sturdy tongs, a fat separator, a meat thermometer, and an extra timer.

IN PRAISE OF SLINGS, MITTS, BANDS, AND MORE

Some pressure cooker recipes call for cooking food inside a bowl or baking dish placed inside the pot, forming a sort of pressurized steam oven. It's a great way to cook breakfast casseroles and many desserts. But if you've ever tried to handle a hot dish in a steamy environment, you know that the hardest part of these recipes can be getting the bowl or basket out of the pot. Traditional potholders get wet and hot; silicone mitts are often bulky or slippery.

In some cases, the handles on the trivet that comes with your pot will suffice for lifting. But if the bowl is too deep or large, it's virtually impossible to use them to safely remove the dish. What to do?

The least expensive solution is to create a **foil sling**: Fold a long piece of aluminum foil over itself two or three times to make a sturdy strip. Place the strip under the bowl inside the pot and fold down the top "handles" during cooking. Make sure that the strip is long enough to provide adequate handles at the top and wide enough to allow the bowl to be lifted securely without tipping over. Once you've made a foil sling, you can reuse it many times.

Several commercial products can solve this problem as well—silicone trivets, stretchy silicone bands that go under a bowl, modified tongs that can grab the edges of the bowl—and every Instant Pot® user has a favorite.

What the Buttons Mean

With the wealth of cooking selections, it can be overwhelming to decide which one to use. Here's a quick rundown of what they do.

Most of the settings (**Poultry, Beans/Chili, Soup, Meat**) cook on high pressure for default times, but you can change these, either with Adjust, which changes among three preset times, or with the + and − buttons, which add or subtract time in 1-minute increments. The default times almost never match the exact cooking times I want, so I rarely use them.

➤ The **Manual** setting can be switched to any time and (in all models but the LUX) from low pressure to high pressure. It's the selection I use most, along with Steam.

➤ The **Steam** function heats continuously and thus gets hotter faster than the other settings, which cycle on and off. With 1 cup of water in the pot, for instance, the Steam setting will come to pressure almost a minute faster than the Manual setting. This can be crucial for quick-cooking foods.

➤ The **Multigrain** function has a presoaking time before it starts coming to pressure.

➤ The **Rice** setting cooks on low pressure, and the time is predetermined depending on the amount of rice that is in the pot. It *cannot* be changed.

➤ The **Yogurt** function has two segments, one for heating the milk and one for incubating it.

➤ The **Slow Cook** setting has three temperature selections: Less (low), Normal (medium), and More (high). In the latest version of the DUO model, Slow Cook on Less mode is between 180°F and 190°F (82°C and 87.8°C). Slow Cook on Normal mode is between 190°F and 200°F (87.8°C and 93°C). Slow Cook on More mode is between 200°F and 210°F (93°C and 99°C).

FREQUENTLY ASKED QUESTIONS

When should I use natural release versus quick release?

I try to use natural pressure release for at least 10 to 15 minutes if it can be done without overcooking the dish. I reserve quick release for dishes that require very short cooking times, such as fish, eggs, and tender vegetables or other foods that easily overcook. (I speed it up even more by placing a cold, wet cloth on the lid opposite the pressure release valve, and topping that with a small sealed bag of ice. This method can also be used during natural release to lessen the time it takes.) Quick release is also useful when a dish cooks in stages—if, for instance, the meat component needs to cook longer than the vegetables, I quick release the pressure at the end of the first cooking time, and sometimes the second time as well.

Shouldn't meats always be finished with natural pressure release?

If there's one thing I read constantly from online discussion groups for the Instant Pot®, it's that you should never use quick release with meat, because it makes meat dry or tough (or both). It's simply not true. Overcooking meat makes it dry. Depending on the cut, overcooking or undercooking can leave it tough. Period. I've done side-by-side comparisons with pork tenderloin, chicken breast, and chuck (beef shoulder), using a slightly longer cooking time with a quick release on half and a shorter cooking time with some natural release with the other half. I tried as much as possible to compare equal-size pieces of meat, and served them at the same internal temperature. I served guests both, and no one could tell the difference. Use whichever fits with your recipe and cooking schedule.

How full can I fill the pot? To the MAX line?

That depends on how you're using the pot. It's fine to fill it to the MAX line if you're slow cooking, but not if you're pressure cooking. In my opinion, the lack of markings for correct pressure cooking levels is the single biggest flaw of the Instant Pot®. For safe and effective pressure cooking, you should never fill the pot more than about two-thirds full. That goes for liquid or semiliquid foods like stews, soups, and stocks. If you're steaming vegetables or meat, or making a cheesecake, don't worry if the solid food or the cheese-cake pan extends up past the two-thirds mark. When you're cooking foods that foam up, like beans, or foods that expand, like pasta, don't go above half full.

Cooking under pressure with a full pot causes three possible problems: First, it can take so long to come to pressure that the pot shuts down; second, it can bubble up and clog the steam valve, causing the pot to overheat and shut down; and third, even after a complete pressure release, the liquid can boil quite vigorously and overflow or even erupt out of the pot when opened.

Can I pressure cook pasta and oatmeal?

While the manual recommends against pressure cooking a long list of foods, such as oatmeal, applesauce, and pasta. However, to my knowledge, the Instant Pot® is the only electric (or stove top) pressure cooker with such a stricture, and my guess is that it's added for reasons of liability. While I am not usually one to advise ignoring a manual, in this case I do, and I base my opinion on years of pressure cooking in various models of cookers, and on what the manuals of similar pressure cookers state. That said, you should never fill the pressure cooker more than half full with these types of foods; I rarely fill it more than one-third full with them.

Can I substitute one cut of meat for another? Pork loin for pork shoulder, for instance, or chicken breasts for chicken thighs?

Different meats have varying amounts of connective tissue and fat, which means that they cook at different rates. Substituting one for another is usually possible—it just requires a shorter or longer cooking time. In those cases, refer to a recipe that gives you a reliable cooking time for the cut you have. However, trying to follow a particular recipe with a different cut is usually a bad idea. See the sections on The Best Chicken Ever (page 25) and Choosing Meat (page 26).

How can I adapt a recipe for the Instant Pot®?

Any recipe that uses wet cooking methods (soups, stews, braises, steaming) can be converted pretty easily. Most recipes for slow cookers are fine cooked under pressure. The best way to adapt a recipe is to look up a reliable pressure cooker recipe that's similar to what you want to do, and use the cooking time and directions you find there.

But, unfortunately, some recipes can't be adapted. Anything that relies heavily on dry heat (roasting or baking) or frying isn't a great candidate for pressure cooking or slow cooking. You can sometimes achieve a similar flavor, but the texture will not be the same.

How much liquid do I need? What kind can I use?

A good rule of thumb is to use at least 1 cup of liquid in any recipe, but that amount can include the liquid that's released by meat or poultry as it cooks, so you don't always have to start out with a full cup. For instance, 3 pounds of chuck will release about 2 cups of liquid as it cooks (partially fat and partially water based). Dry ingredients like pasta or beans obviously need enough liquid to rehydrate, but how much will depend on what the finished dish is. In general, using too much liquid is better than too little, since you can pour off or boil off excess liquid after cooking.

As for what kinds of liquids, there's a misconception in discussion groups that only stock or water counts toward that 1 cup of liquid. Users seem especially wary of using tomato or dairy products, but I use these frequently. While I wouldn't count thick tomato paste as part of my liquid, I often use diced tomatoes with their juice or strained tomatoes for some or all of my liquid. And if the recipe warrants it, I use milk, cream, and evaporated milk with no problems.

Can I use thickening agents in my sauces?

Yes—but not all thickeners, and not a lot. Cornstarch can break down at long cooking times and extremely high temperatures, so it's best saved for adding after pressure cooking. Dredging meats in flour or building a roux with fat and flour is fine so long as the resulting sauce is thin enough to flow easily and you scrape up any browned bits from the bottom of the pot. Also, keep in mind that you can thicken sauces after cooking simply by boiling off some of the excess water, which will also deepen the flavor.

My sealing ring smells like curry/garlic/chile/etc. How can I get rid of the odor?

What helps the most is to remove the sealing ring every time you use your pot and wash and dry it, either by hand or in the dishwasher. Then, leave it out of the lid to air out. Some cooks swear by leaving it in the sun, keeping it in the freezer, or storing it in a bag of ground coffee. I don't find that these help much, but then I don't notice any transfer of flavors from my ring. Some people may be more sensitive to smells, and if that's the case with you, then you might want to buy an extra ring (or two). Many people recommend using one ring exclusively for savory dishes and the other for sweet dishes.

PRESSURE COOKING AT HIGH ALTITUDE

If you remember your science lessons, you know that the higher the altitude, the lower the atmospheric pressure. For the cook, one thing this means is that the higher the altitude, the lower the boiling point of water (and other liquids), and the faster it evaporates. With slight changes in altitude, the difference is negligible, but when you get high enough (above 2,000 feet), it can be significant. While the sealed interior of a pressure cooker helps make up for the lower atmospheric pressure, you'll still have to make some adjustments if you live in the mountains. Most pressure cooker manufacturers recommend increasing cooking times by 5 percent for every 1,000 feet above 2,000 feet (so a dish that cooks under pressure for 20 minutes at sea level would cook for 21 minutes at 3,000 feet or for 22 minutes at 4,000 feet). Some also recommend increasing the amount of liquid slightly.

A PLENTIFUL PANTRY

Most cooks have a pantry (either an actual pantry or just a few shelves in a cabinet) that contains the ingredients they use regularly. I take the concept of a pantry a step further and use it to include refrigerator and freezer staples. Your pantry will depend on the cuisines you like to cook (Asian recipes call for different ingredients than Mexican, for instance) as well as your personal tastes. The recipes in this book cross geographical boundaries and call upon various flavor profiles; what follows is a partial list of the staples my recipes call for.

SHELF STAPLES

- **DRY BEANS** (pinto, black, cannellini, chickpeas, lentils, etc.)
- **RICE** (long-grain white, brown, basmati, Arborio, etc.)
- **PASTA** (farfalle, penne, shells, orzo, etc.)
- **CANNED DICED TOMATOES** (I like fire roasted, but any type will work.)
- **STRAINED TOMATOES OR TOMATO SAUCE** (Strained tomatoes are similar to tomato sauce, but they aren't cooked before canning, so they're fresher tasting than tomato sauce. I like Pomi brand.)
- **HOISIN SAUCE**
- **SOY SAUCE**
- **OYSTER SAUCE**

- **ASIAN CHILI GARLIC SAUCE** (such as the Lee Kum Kee brand)
- **VINEGAR** (rice, apple cider, and sherry)
- **EXTRA-VIRGIN OLIVE OIL**
- **HOT SAUCE, SUCH AS TABASCO**
- **CANNED CHIPOTLES IN ADOBO** (My recipes call for *chipotle purée*. I recommend puréeing the whole can, transferring the purée to a plastic container, and storing it in the refrigerator. It lasts indefinitely, and it's much easier to measure out.)
- **CANNED GREEN CHILES** (such as the Hatch brand)
- **ROASTED RED PEPPERS**
- **DRY RED WINE, DRY WHITE WINE, AND DRY SHERRY**

SPICES (BEYOND THE USUAL)

- ➤ KOSHER SALT (My recipes are developed with Diamond brand kosher salt, which is coarser than table salt. If you use table salt, cut the salt in my recipes by about half.)

- ➤ BLACK PEPPERCORNS FOR FRESHLY GROUND BLACK PEPPER
- ➤ SWEET (NOT HOT) SMOKED PAPRIKA
- ➤ FRESH NUTMEG
- ➤ CAJUN SEASONING MIX

REFRIGERATOR

- ➤ UNSALTED BUTTER
- ➤ HEAVY (WHIPPING) CREAM
- ➤ WHOLE MILK
- ➤ SOUR CREAM

- ➤ PARMESAN OR SIMILAR CHEESE (It doesn't have to be imported Parmigiano-Reggiano; there are good domestic versions available.)

FREEZER

- ➤ IQF (INDIVIDUALLY QUICK FROZEN) SHELL-ON SHRIMP
- ➤ FROZEN TILAPIA OR COD FILLETS

- ➤ ORANGE JUICE CONCENTRATE

MOVING PAST PRESSURE

It's undeniable that the most popular function of the Instant Pot® is pressure cooking—that's what gives the appliance its name, after all. But savvy cooks don't discount the other features. Even those who never considered making their own yogurt have succumbed to the ease of homemade. One pot, two steps, and into the refrigerator it goes. What could it be easier?

The slow cooker function might seem old-fashioned, but many cooks have favorite recipes designed for the slow cooker, and they don't want to give them up. With an Instant Pot®, you can keep your slow cooker favorites but ditch the slow cooker! And slow cooking in the pot has a big advantage over conventional cookers: You can brown meats or sweat vegetables right in the pot rather than having to dirty more pots and pans.

BEANS AND RICE AND EGGS— OH, MY!

To enter into the pressure cooking world, two of the foods most users cook first are beans and rice. And if there's more of a gateway Instant Pot® food than hard-boiled eggs, I don't know what it is. Here are a few guidelines to get the best out of these popular foods.

Beans

While you can cook dry, unsoaked beans relatively quickly in the pot (and occasionally I call for them in this cookbook), I'm a firm believer in soaking most beans in salted water anywhere from 6 hours to overnight. I know—it requires planning ahead. But not only does it allow for faster cooking, it also produces a superior dish. Soaked beans will be seasoned and tender, with intact skins and virtually no broken beans. It takes 2 minutes, tops, in the morning before you go to work. You can even measure out your beans and prepare the soaking water (1 tablespoon kosher salt or 1½ teaspoons table salt, dissolved in 1 quart of water) the night before, and just combine them before running out the door.

Rice

One of the dedicated functions of the Instant Pot® is the rice cooker function, which is, unfortunately, not explained very well in the manual. Despite that, it's a handy setting under the right circumstances. It's best reserved for long-grain white rice, and works best with 1 cup or more of raw rice. For best results, measure out 1 part rice to 1¼ parts water, and add 1 teaspoon kosher salt and 2 teaspoons unsalted butter per cup of uncooked rice. Hit the Rice button, and the Instant Pot® will take care of the rest. If you choose not to use the Rice setting, you can cook all kinds of rice with either high or low pressure, plain or with additions. For very small amounts, you can cook rice in a bowl inside the pot. Try a couple of recipes and see what works best for you.

Eggs

It sometimes seems that what excites new users the most is making hard-boiled eggs in the pot. Certainly, if you've never steamed eggs before, it's a revelation; they practically peel themselves. But if you read instructions for pressure cooking eggs on websites and in online discussions, you can end up more confused than when you started. Because the size of the pot, the amount of water, and the temperature of the eggs all play a role in how quickly they cook, different users get different results and swear by different methods. I give my methods for soft- and hard-boiled eggs on pages 34 and 35, and I believe they're the best place to start.

THE BEST CHICKEN EVER

It's no secret that recipes for chicken are among the most popular in cookbooks, blogs, and websites. What's not to like? Chicken is versatile, it cooks quickly, and it's inexpensive. As popular as it is, though, there's a lot of misinformation about cooking it, which means people everywhere are eating sad, overcooked chicken. But you don't have to be one of those people! A little knowledge and a few tips will put you on the path to the best chicken ever.

Breasts

Breasts, especially if skinless, contain very little fat, so they dry out very easily. The goal for whole breast pieces (whether boneless or bone-in) is to cook them through while leaving them moist and tender. It's not impossible, but it does mean discarding a piece of advice you've probably heard your entire cooking life—that you should always cook chicken to 165°F.

The USDA gives that advice as an absolute, but it turns out that cooking chicken so that it's safe (pathogen-free, that is) is a function of both temperature and time, not just temperature. While an internal temperature of 165°F will kill 99 percent of pathogens instantly, it turns out that if you keep your chicken at 150°F for about 2 minutes, the same number of pathogens will bite the dust. Fortunately for us, that's not hard to do, and chicken breasts cooked to 150°F are much more palatable than those cooked to 165°F.

Bite-size pieces of chicken breast cook so quickly that I don't recommend trying to pressure cook them.

Thighs and Legs

The same times and temperatures hold for the safety of chicken thighs and legs, but those pieces have enough fat and connective tissue that they are better at 165°F than at 150°F. What this means is that you can't substitute breasts for thighs without changing the cooking time or temperature. That's not too difficult with conventional cooking methods, but in the Instant Pot®, where cooking happens quickly, it's more problematic. If you want to substitute whole breasts for whole thighs in the recipes in this book, follow the timing for Perfect Chicken Breast on page 140.

Whole Chicken

For whole chickens, most pressure cooker recipes call for way too much cooking time. "Falling-apart" chicken seems to be what many cooks strive for, but in my opinion a chicken that's falling apart is a chicken that's overdone. For my preferred method for pressure cooking a whole chicken, see the recipe for Milk-Braised Chicken with Lemon-Garlic Sauce on page 148.

CHOOSING MEAT

Pressure cookers excel at cooking tougher cuts of meat, such as beef or pork shoulder, ribs, lamb shanks, or oxtails. Probably the two most popular cuts are beef shoulder (also called chuck roast or steak) and pork shoulder (also called pork butt and, when cut into strips, country-style ribs). These are the meats that can be shredded for carnitas, pulled pork, or barbecued beef sandwiches. They can also be cubed and cooked in stews and chilis, or left whole and cooked as roasts.

That's not to say that leaner, more tender cuts—such as sirloin, pork tenderloin, and pork loin—can't be cooked under pressure. They just take more attention and much less time. The problem arises when an inexperienced cook uses a tender, lean cut in a recipe designed for a tougher cut, or vice versa. I can't count the number of times I've seen questions about how to turn a pork tenderloin into carnitas. A tenderloin that can be shredded is a sadly overcooked tenderloin. Think of it as very expensive pork leather.

And while we're on the subject of pork tenderloin, it's a different cut of meat from the pork loin. Both are very lean cuts, but their different shapes mean they cook at very different rates. A tenderloin is a long, thin single muscle. A pork loin roast is thicker and shorter, and can include a couple of different muscles. Both can be cooked in the pressure cooker (see Pork Loin Braised in Milk on page 180 and Pork Tenderloin with Cabbage and Noodles on page 178), but they can't be substituted for each other. And neither cut should ever be substituted for pork butt.

Know the Part

One big problem with pressure cooking meat comes from recipe writers, not cooks. Too many times, recipes call for nonspecific terms like "pot roast" or "pork roast" or "beef roast." If it's not clear what part of the animal the "roast" is supposed to come from, you'll never know how to cook it so it can be its best. Choose recipes that specify where the meat comes from.

THIS BOOK'S RECIPES

The recipes in this book were developed and tested using the 6-quart DUO Instant Pot®. Organizationally, they are mostly divided by the main ingredient, except for three course-driven chapters—Breakfast, Vegetables & Sides, and Desserts—and one final chapter on Kitchen Staples. Each recipe is tagged, if appropriate, with one or more of the following labels:

➤ **DIETARY INFO:** Grain-Free; Dairy-Free

➤ **TIMESAVERS:** 30 Minutes or Less; 60 Minutes or Less

➤ **ONE POT:** Not only can the recipe be made entirely in the pressure cooker, but it makes a complete meal on its own.

Some recipes begin with searing meat or poultry. Usually I give instructions for doing this in the Instant Pot®, but in *some* cases I recommend using a large cast iron or other heavy skillet on the stove instead. Such a skillet has several advantages. First, it will heat more evenly since the bottom is flat (the Instant Pot® line is slightly convex). Second, it's easier to turn meat, especially a whole chicken, in a shallower vessel. Third, since it's larger, you won't have to work in batches when searing a large amount of meat. I think those considerations are worth the extra pan to clean. If you do use a separate pan, do any deglazing (scraping up browned bits) in the skillet and transfer the liquid to the Instant Pot®.

To the side of each recipe, there's an "at a glance" panel that indicates prep and finishing time, pressure time and level, release method, and total time.

Prep and Finishing time includes tasks like mixing, searing, or sautéing ingredients, finishing sauces, browning meats, and the like. The *Total Time* is the total of prep and finishing time, time under pressure, and release time, plus the 5 to 10 minutes needed for the unit to come to pressure. I've tried to be as accurate as possible, but the times can vary depending on many factors, including different Instant Pot® models.

If you would like to double a recipe, make sure that the total volume in the pot doesn't exceed two-thirds. Keep in mind that a larger volume of liquid will take longer to come to pressure, so the total time in the recipe will not be accurate.

Some of the recipes include tips, which may include alternative ingredients, information about unusual ingredients or techniques, timesaving steps, or extra steps to improve flavor or texture.

Each recipe gives nutritional information per serving. In the case of recipes with ingredients list variations, nutritional information will also be provided for each meal variation. Most of the recipes in this book make 4 servings, but some make 6. For main dishes, the serving sizes are generous; if your family has smaller appetites, my recipes might yield more than the specified number of servings.

PREP AND
FINISHING
20 minutes

MANUAL
8 minutes high
pressure

RELEASE
Quick

**TOTAL TIME
35 MINUTES**

30 MIN OR LESS

60 MIN OR LESS

ONE POT

GRAIN-FREE

DAIRY-FREE

Notes on Ingredients

With very few exceptions, I specify kosher salt in my recipes. I use Diamond brand kosher salt; if you use table salt or other fine salt, use half the amount specified.

I use unsalted butter in my recipes, but you can use salted butter instead; if so, you may wish to add less salt to the recipe than what it calls for.

For chicken or vegetable stock, if you are not using homemade (from the recipes on pages 228 and 229), choose a can or box of low-sodium stock, or reduce the amount of salt in the recipe by about one-third.

POACHED EGGS (PAGE 36)

CHAPTER 2

BREAKFAST

Whether you want a quick weekday breakfast or a leisurely weekend brunch dish, the Instant Pot® is the perfect tool to get you going in the morning. Eggs—hard-boiled, soft-boiled, or poached—are a breeze to cook, and peel! If oatmeal is your breakfast of choice, the pot will be your best morning friend. When you have a little more time, or want a fancier breakfast dish, a strata, quiche, or breakfast casserole makes a delicious alternative. All you need is a heat-proof dish that holds 4 to 6 cups and fits in your pot. Or you can make individual quiches or French toast in 1-cup ramekins or custard cups. Either way, special breakfasts don't get any easier!

FRENCH TOAST CUPS

It might seem odd to use a pressure cooker for French toast, but not only is the French toast great tasting, this method is much less messy than making it the traditional way. It also yields perfectly uniform servings without having to time how long the bread is in the egg mixture. As a plus, you can make these cups ahead of time and refrigerate them. To serve, heat them for a minute in a microwave, then sauté in butter to crisp up and finish heating through. **SERVES 4**

PREP AND FINISHING
15 minutes

STEAM
8 minutes
high pressure

RELEASE
Natural for 5 minutes

**TOTAL TIME
30 MINUTES**

30 MIN OR LESS

3 tablespoons unsalted butter, divided

2 large eggs

1 cup whole milk

¼ cup heavy (whipping) cream

¼ teaspoon vanilla extract

1 teaspoon orange juice concentrate

Pinch salt

4 cups (¾-inch) bread cubes (4 to 5 bread slices)

1 cup water, for steaming

1. Prepare the ramekins. Using about 1 tablespoon of butter, coat the bottoms and sides of 4 small (1- to 1½-cup) ramekins or custard cups.

2. Make the French toast mixture. In a large bowl, whisk the eggs until the yolks and whites are completely mixed. Add the milk, cream, vanilla, orange juice concentrate, and salt and whisk to combine. Add the bread cubes and gently stir to coat with the egg mixture. Let sit for 2 to 3 minutes to let the bread absorb some of the custard, then gently stir again. Spoon the bread mixture evenly into the cups. Cover each cup with aluminum foil.

3. **Pressure cook.** Pour the water into the pot. Place a trivet in the pot and place the ramekins on top, stacking them if necessary. Lock the lid into place. Select Steam; adjust the pressure to High and the time to 8 minutes. After cooking, let the pressure release naturally for 5 minutes, then quick release any remaining pressure. Unlock and remove the lid and use tongs to remove the French toast cups.

4. **Finish the French toast.** Remove the foil and let the French toasts cool for a few minutes. While they cool, melt the remaining 2 tablespoons of butter in a large skillet or griddle. Unmold the French toasts. When the butter has just stopped foaming, place the French toasts in the skillet and cook until golden brown, about 2 minutes. Turn and brown the other side, 1 to 2 minutes more. Serve immediately.

PER SERVING Calories: 195; Fat: 15g; Sodium: 239mg; Carbohydrates: 9g; Fiber: 1g; Protein: 6g

SOFT-BOILED EGGS

I loved soft-boiled eggs when I was little. On weekends, my mother would put them in the cute eggcups she'd inherited from her mother, and carefully cut off the tops so we could scoop out the soft eggs with our spoons. On weekdays, when we were more rushed, she'd crack the cooked eggs, remove them from the shell, and cut them up on toast. No matter how you like your soft-boiled eggs—super soft in the shell or a little firmer on toast—you can get exactly what you want just by changing the pressure and cooking time. **SERVES 4**

PREP AND FINISHING
3 minutes

STEAM
3 minutes low pressure (soft eggs) or 2 minutes high pressure (slightly firmer eggs)

RELEASE
Quick

TOTAL TIME
10 MINUTES

30 MIN OR LESS

GRAIN-FREE

DAIRY-FREE

4 large eggs, refrigerator temperature

1 cup water, for steaming

Toast, for serving (optional)

1. Make an ice bath. Fill a medium bowl about halfway with cold water. Add a handful of ice cubes. Set aside.

2. Place the eggs in the pot. Pour the water into the Instant Pot® and place a steamer trivet or basket inside. Place the eggs on the steamer.

3. Pressure cook the eggs. Lock the lid into place. *For soft eggs:* Select Steam; adjust the pressure to Low and the time to 3 minutes. *For slightly firmer eggs:* Select Steam; adjust the pressure to High and the time to 2 minutes. After cooking, quick release the pressure. Unlock and remove the lid and use tongs to transfer the eggs to the ice bath.

4. Finish and serve. Leave the eggs in the ice bath until just cool enough to handle, about 30 seconds. *For soft eggs:* Place the eggs in eggcups. Use a sharp knife or egg topper to cut the tops off the eggs. Serve immediately. *For slightly firmer eggs:* Working quickly, gently crack the shell and peel each egg. Serve immediately over toast.

COOKING TIP: While it's very easy to cook double the number of eggs, it's difficult to top or peel more than four eggs and serve them while they're still warm, unless you have a helper.

PER SERVING Calories: 71; Fat: 5g; Sodium: 70mg; Carbohydrates: 0g; Fiber: 0g; Protein: 6g

HARD-BOILED EGGS

When it comes to quick breakfasts, it doesn't get quicker than a hard-boiled egg. Pressure steaming eggs makes them a cinch to peel, which means it's even easier to grab a high-protein breakfast to go. And don't stop with plain eggs. Maybe you don't think of egg salad and deviled eggs for breakfast, but you should—they're tasty and filling choices to start your morning. Consider making a batch or two of hard-boiled eggs on the weekend to have on hand for meals or snacks throughout the week. **SERVES 4**

PREP AND FINISHING
3 minutes

STEAM
4 minutes
high pressure

RELEASE
Quick

TOTAL TIME
10 MINUTES

30 MIN OR LESS

GRAIN-FREE

DAIRY-FREE

4 large eggs, refrigerator temperature

1 cup water, for steaming

1. **Make an ice bath.** Fill a medium bowl about halfway with cold water. Add several handfuls of ice cubes. Set aside.

2. **Place the eggs in the pot.** Pour the water into the Instant Pot® and place a steamer trivet or basket inside. Place the eggs on the steamer.

3. **Pressure cook the eggs.** Lock the lid into place. Select Steam; adjust the pressure to High and the time to 4 minutes. After cooking, quick release the pressure. Unlock and remove the lid and use tongs to transfer the eggs to the ice bath.

4. **Serve the eggs.** For warm eggs, remove from the ice bath as soon as they're cool enough to handle. Peel and serve. For cold eggs, leave them in the ice bath until thoroughly chilled, 10 to 15 minutes. Peel and serve.

COOKING TIP: There's a window of several minutes for pressure-steamed eggs without overcooking them, which causes a green ring to form around the yolk. If you want to make sure the yolks are completely dry and pale yellow, you may wish to add 1 minute to the steaming time. If you prefer eggs with yolks that are set but still soft in the center, subtract 1 minute.

PER SERVING Calories: 71; Fat: 5g; Sodium: 70mg; Carbohydrates: 0g; Fiber: 0g; Protein: 6g

POACHED EGGS

I've seen a lot of recipes for "poached" eggs in pressure cookers, but without exception, they are not true poached eggs. Cracking an egg into a cup and steaming it is a great way to cook eggs, but it's not poaching. But you *can* use your Instant Pot® to poach eggs. Use the Sauté function to heat the poaching liquid, and with a few tips, a couple of pieces of equipment, and a little practice, you'll be able to produce gorgeous, perfectly cooked poached eggs. **SERVES 4**

PREP
10 minutes

POACH
4 minutes

TOTAL TIME
15 MINUTES

30 MIN OR LESS

GRAIN-FREE

DAIRY-FREE

2 quarts water

2 tablespoons table salt

1 tablespoon white vinegar

4 large eggs

Buttered toast or English muffins, for serving (optional)

1. Heat the poaching liquid. Pour the water into the Instant Pot® and add the salt and vinegar. (The combination of acid and salt acts on the alkaline whites and brings the eggs to the surface of the water as they cook so they cook evenly.) Select Sauté and adjust to More for high heat. As the water heats, stir to dissolve the salt. Heat the water to just below the boiling point—between 200°F and 205°F.

2. Prepare the eggs. Place a small strainer over a custard cup or ramekin. Crack an egg into the strainer and let it sit for a couple of minutes to drain off the thin egg whites. (This makes a neater-looking poached egg, as it's the thin whites that fly around in the water.) Gently tip the egg in the strainer into a new custard cup. Repeat with the remaining eggs, placing each egg in a separate cup.

3. **Poach the eggs.** When the water has heated, tip the eggs, one at a time, from the cup into the water, spacing the eggs evenly and keeping track of the order in which you put them in the water. Cook each egg for 3½ to 4 minutes. Use a large slotted spoon to remove the eggs. Drain briefly on paper towels.

4. **Serve the eggs:** Place the eggs in cups or on buttered toast or English muffins (if using) to serve.

SERVING TIP: If you make your toast while the water is heating and the eggs are draining, you can keep it on a rack in a low oven or warming drawer while you cook the eggs. That way, you'll have warm toast and hot eggs at the same time.

PER SERVING Calories: 71; Fat: 5g; Sodium: 167mg; Carbohydrates: 0g; Fiber: 0g; Protein: 6g

MAPLE SAUSAGE BREAKFAST CASSEROLE

When I was growing up, sausage and French toast was a special breakfast reserved for Sundays. I loved the combination of the savory sausage and the sweet maple syrup that coated the toast, and honestly, I've never really outgrown my taste for that childhood meal. This recipe combines those two favorites in one dish, and pressure cooking makes it fast enough for a weekday morning. Who wants to wait for Sunday morning? **SERVES 4**

PREP AND FINISHING
10 minutes

MANUAL
10 minutes high pressure

RELEASE
Natural for 10 minutes

TOTAL TIME
35 MINUTES

60 MIN OR LESS

ONE POT

8 ounces breakfast sausage, removed from its casings

3 large eggs

1 cup whole milk

½ teaspoon kosher salt

¼ cup plus 1 tablespoon pure maple syrup, divided

3 cups (1-inch) stale bread cubes (3 to 4 bread slices)

1 teaspoon unsalted butter

1 cup water, for steaming

1. **Brown the sausage.** Preheat the Instant Pot® by selecting Sauté and adjust to Normal for medium heat. Put the sausage in the pot, breaking it up with a spatula into bite-size pieces. Cook, stirring frequently, until the sausage pieces are browned. Don't worry if the sausage isn't cooked all the way through; it will cook again. Remove the sausage and rinse out the inner pot, scraping off any browned bits.

2. **Prepare the remaining ingredients.** In a medium bowl, whisk the eggs, then add the milk, salt, and 1 tablespoon of maple syrup and whisk to combine. Add the bread cubes and gently stir to coat them with the egg mixture. Let sit for 2 to 3 minutes to let the bread absorb some of the custard, then gently stir again. Add the sausage and gently stir to combine with the bread.

3. **Prepare the casserole.** Coat the bottom and sides of a 1-quart baking dish with the butter. Pour the bread and sausage mixture into the baking dish and lay a square of aluminum foil over the top of the dish. Do not crimp the foil down because the casserole will expand as it cooks; you just want to keep moisture off the top.

4. Pressure cook. Pour the water into the Instant Pot®. Place a trivet with handles in the pot and place the baking dish on top. If your trivet doesn't have handles, use a foil sling (see page 16) to make removing the dish easier. Lock the lid into place. Select Manual; adjust the pressure to High and the time to 10 minutes. After cooking, let the pressure release naturally for 10 minutes, then quick release any remaining pressure. Unlock and remove the lid.

5. Finish the casserole. Carefully remove the baking dish from the pot. Remove the foil and drizzle the remaining ¼ cup of maple syrup over the top. Let the casserole cool for a few minutes, then serve.

SERVING TIP: If you like, after drizzling it with maple syrup, place the casserole under a preheated broiler for a few minutes to crisp the top.

PER SERVING Calories: 368; Fat: 22g; Sodium: 861mg; Carbohydrates: 25g; Fiber: 1g; Protein: 18g

STEEL-CUT OATMEAL
THREE WAYS

If you thought you were doomed to instant oatmeal in the mornings, just wait until you try steel-cut oats from the pressure cooker. You'll trade in instant oatmeal for the Instant Pot® in no time at all. Toasting the oats in butter before cooking makes them extra nutty and delicious, but if you're in a rush, skip that step, and you'll still be able to enjoy a nutritious warm breakfast even on the busiest of mornings. **SERVES 4**

PREP AND FINISHING
10 minutes

MANUAL
10 minutes
high pressure

RELEASE
Natural for 10 minutes

**TOTAL TIME
35 MINUTES**

60 MIN OR LESS

ONE POT

CORE INGREDIENTS
2 tablespoons unsalted butter

1 cup steel-cut oats

1 tablespoon granulated sugar, plus more for serving

¼ teaspoon kosher salt

2 cups water

1 cup whole milk, plus more for serving

FOR CINNAMON-RAISIN OATMEAL
½ cup raisins

1 teaspoon ground cinnamon

1 tablespoon brown sugar

FOR ALMOND-DATE OATMEAL
½ teaspoon vanilla extract

½ cup toasted chopped almonds

½ cup chopped dates

FOR NUTELLA-BANANA OATMEAL
½ cup Nutella or other chocolate-hazelnut spread

2 ripe bananas, sliced

1. Brown the oats. Preheat the Instant Pot® by selecting Sauté and adjust to More for high heat. Put the butter in the pot to melt. When the butter has stopped foaming, add the oats and stir them to coat with the butter. Continue cooking, stirring frequently, until the oats smell nutty, 2 to 3 minutes. ➤

PER SERVING Calories: 176;
Fat: 9g; Sodium: 214mg;
Carbohydrates: 20g;
Fiber: 2g; Protein: 5g

PER SERVING (CINNAMON-RAISIN VARIATION) Calories: 240;
Fat: 9g; Sodium: 216mg;
Carbohydrates: 37g;
Fiber: 3g; Protein: 5g

PER SERVING (ALMOND-DATE VARIATION) Calories: 309;
Fat: 15g; Sodium: 214mg;
Carbohydrates: 39g;
Fiber: 5g; Protein: 8g

PER SERVING (NUTELLA-BANANA VARIATION) Calories: 429;
Fat: 20g; Sodium: 230mg;
Carbohydrates: 56g;
Fiber: 6g; Protein: 7g

2. **Prepare the remaining ingredients.** Add the sugar, salt, water, and milk and stir to combine.

For Cinnamon-Raisin Oatmeal: Stir in the raisins and cinnamon.

For Almond-Date Oatmeal: Stir in the vanilla.

3. **Pressure cook.** Lock the lid into place. Select Manual; adjust the pressure to High and the time to 10 minutes. After cooking, let the pressure release naturally for 10 minutes, then quick release any remaining pressure. Unlock and remove the lid.

4. **Finish the oatmeal.** Stir the oatmeal and spoon it into four bowls. Stir in the remaining ingredients, depending on which variation you chose. Adjust to your taste, adding extra milk or sugar if you like, and serve.

INDIVIDUAL SPINACH QUICHES
IN HAM CUPS

These mini quiches cook much faster than the full-size version (page 46), so you can easily make them on weekday mornings (especially if you prep all the ingredients the night before). With more eggs in proportion to the dairy, they're also sturdier—which makes them perfect for a breakfast on the go. They're a tasty alternative to plain eggs for those mornings when you want a change. **SERVES 4**

PREP
10 minutes

STEAM
7 minutes
high pressure

RELEASE
Quick

**TOTAL TIME
25 MINUTES**

30 MIN OR LESS

GRAIN-FREE

4 thin slices deli ham

¼ cup frozen spinach, thawed and well drained

½ cup shredded Cheddar cheese (about 2 ounces)

4 large eggs

¼ cup milk

¼ cup heavy (whipping) cream

½ teaspoon kosher salt

1 cup water, for steaming

1. Prepare the ramekins. Place a slice of ham in each of 4 small (1- to 1½-cup) ramekins or custard cups and press it into the bottom and up the sides to form a cup shape. Divide the spinach and cheese among the ramekins.

2. Make the quiches. In a medium bowl, whisk the eggs, then add the milk, cream, and salt and whisk to combine. Pour the custard evenly into the ramekins.

3. Pressure cook. Pour the water into the Instant Pot®. Place a trivet in the pot and place the ramekins on top, stacking if necessary. Place a piece of foil over the ramekins to keep water out of the quiches. Lock the lid into place. Select Steam; adjust the pressure to High and the time to 7 minutes. After cooking, quick release the pressure. Unlock and remove the lid.

4. Serve the quiches. Use tongs to carefully remove the ramekins from the pot. Let them cool for a few minutes, then serve.

PER SERVING Calories: 199; Fat: 15g; Sodium: 817mg; Carbohydrates: 3g; Fiber: 0g; Protein: 14g

CINNAMON-APPLE STRATA

The main difference between a "breakfast casserole" and a "strata" is how the ingredients are mixed and placed in the baking dish. In a casserole, they're all tossed together and spooned or poured into the dish. In a strata, the custard-soaked bread is layered separately from the other ingredients. I like the layers of apples in this recipe, but if you prefer, you can make this casserole style. **SERVES 4**

PREP AND FINISHING
10 minutes

MANUAL
10 minutes
high pressure

RELEASE
Natural for 10 minutes

**TOTAL TIME
35 MINUTES**

60 MIN OR LESS

1 large apple, such as Gala, Braeburn, or Granny Smith, peeled, cored, and diced

8 tablespoons brown sugar, divided

2 teaspoons ground cinnamon, divided

3 large eggs

1 cup whole milk

½ teaspoon kosher salt

3 cups (1-inch) stale bread cubes (3 to 4 bread slices)

1 teaspoon unsalted butter, at room temperature

1 cup water, for steaming

1. Prepare the apples. In a small bowl, toss the apple with 2 tablespoons of brown sugar and ½ teaspoon of cinnamon.

2. Prepare the remaining ingredients. In a medium bowl, whisk the eggs, then add the milk, salt, 2 tablespoons of brown sugar, and ½ teaspoon of cinnamon and whisk to combine. Add the bread cubes and gently stir to coat with the egg mixture. Let sit for 2 to 3 minutes to let the bread absorb some of the custard, then gently stir again.

3. Assemble the strata. Coat the bottom and sides of a 1-quart baking dish with the butter. Spoon about a third of the custard and bread mixture into the dish. Spoon about a third of the apples over the bread. Repeat with a third of the bread mixture and a third of the apples, then finish with a final layer of both. Lay a square of aluminum foil over the top of the dish. Do not crimp the foil down because the strata will expand as it cooks; you just want to keep moisture off the top.

4. Pressure cook. Pour the water into the Instant Pot®. Place a trivet with handles in the pot and place the baking dish on top. If your trivet doesn't have handles, use a foil sling (see page 16) to make removing the dish easier. Lock the lid into place. Select Manual; adjust the pressure to High and the time to 10 minutes. After cooking, let the pressure release naturally for 10 minutes, then quick release any remaining pressure. Unlock and remove the lid.

5. Mix the topping and preheat the broiler. While the strata cooks, mix the remaining 4 tablespoons of brown sugar and 1 teaspoon of cinnamon in a small bowl. Turn on the oven to broil.

6. Finish the strata. Carefully remove the baking dish from the pot. Remove the foil and sprinkle the cinnamon-sugar topping over the top of the strata. Place the baking dish under the broiler for several minutes until the top is bubbling. Let cool for a few minutes, then serve.

PER SERVING Calories: 210; Fat: 6g; Sodium: 439mg; Carbohydrates: 34g; Fiber: 2g; Protein: 7g

CRUSTLESS QUICHE LORRAINE

I love traditional quiche, but I don't always have the time to make and bake a crust for it. That's when I turn to this quick version. The trade-off for the crust is not only speed but also an impossibly creamy texture. You can use whatever fillings you like in place of the bacon, onion, and cheese; just make sure that any vegetables are cooked, or they'll add water to the custard, which makes for uneven cooking. **SERVES 4**

PREP AND FINISHING
15 minutes

MANUAL
10 minutes
high pressure

RELEASE
Natural for 10 minutes

**TOTAL TIME
40 MINUTES**

60 MIN OR LESS

ONE POT

GRAIN-FREE

3 bacon slices, chopped

1 small onion, sliced thin

¾ teaspoon kosher salt, divided

3 large eggs

½ cup whole milk

½ cup heavy (whipping) cream

⅛ teaspoon freshly ground white or black pepper

1 teaspoon unsalted butter, at room temperature

1¼ cups grated Swiss-style cheese (about 3 ounces)

1 cup water, for steaming

1. Sauté the bacon and onion. Preheat the Instant Pot® by selecting Sauté and adjust to Normal for medium heat. Cook the bacon until most of the fat has rendered and the bacon is crisp, about 6 minutes. Use a slotted spoon to remove the bacon, and drain on paper towels, leaving the rendered fat in the pot. Add the onion and sprinkle with ¼ teaspoon of salt. Cook, stirring frequently, until the onion pieces separate and soften, 2 to 3 minutes. Transfer the onion to the paper towels with the bacon. Rinse out the inner pot, scraping off any browned bits.

2. Prepare the custard. In a medium bowl, whisk the eggs, then add the milk, cream, pepper, and remaining ½ teaspoon of salt and whisk to combine.

3. Assemble the quiche. Coat the bottom and sides of a 1-quart baking dish with the butter. Sprinkle half of the cheese over the bottom of the dish. Top with the bacon and onion, then add the remaining cheese. Carefully pour the custard over the cheese. Lay a square of aluminum foil over the top of the baking dish. Do not crimp the foil down because the quiche will expand; you just want to keep moisture off the top.

4. Pressure cook. Pour the water into the Instant Pot®. Place a trivet with handles in the pot and place the baking dish on top. If your trivet doesn't have handles, use a foil sling (see page 16) to make removing the dish easier. Lock the lid into place. Select Manual; adjust the pressure to High and the time to 10 minutes. After cooking, let the pressure release naturally for 10 minutes, then quick release any remaining pressure. Unlock and remove the lid.

5. Serve the quiche. Carefully remove the quiche from the pot. Let the quiche cool and set for about 10 minutes before slicing and serving.

SERVING TIP: While quiche from the pressure cooker is wonderfully smooth and creamy, it looks pale compared with an oven-baked quiche. For a nicer presentation, sprinkle additional cheese over the top of the quiche when it comes out of the pot and place it under a preheated broiler for a minutes or two, until the cheese is browned and bubbling.

PER SERVING Calories: 377; Fat: 29g; Sodium: 1068mg; Carbohydrates: 7g; Fiber: 1g; Protein: 23g

QUINOA AND CORN SOUP (PAGE 65)

CHAPTER 3
VEGETABLES & SIDES

You might be so consumed with cooking main dishes that you don't consider pressure cooking vegetables and sides. Don't fall into this trap! With the help of a few tips, you can cook most vegetables perfectly under pressure, from tender beans to sturdier squashes and beets. Since they require little prep and no attention, you can add them to the pot, set it, and turn your attention to other elements of your meal.

Do keep in mind that many vegetables require very little time under pressure. Follow the times, settings, and liquid amounts carefully so you don't overcook or undercook them.

ASPARAGUS ENDS SOUP

I love asparagus, but snapping off the ends—where they start to get tough—can leave a lot of asparagus, which I hate to waste. That's when this soup comes to the rescue. I save up the asparagus ends in the freezer until I have a big bag and then use them in this soup. Pressure cooking coaxes tons of flavor from the tough ends, so all our asparagus can be put to good use. **SERVES 4**

PREP AND FINISHING
15 minutes

MANUAL
10 minutes
high pressure

RELEASE
Natural for 10 minutes

**TOTAL TIME
35 MINUTES**

60 MIN OR LESS

GRAIN-FREE

3 tablespoons unsalted butter

1 medium onion, sliced thin

1½ teaspoons kosher salt, plus more to taste

⅔ cup dry white wine or vermouth

1½ pounds asparagus ends

3 cups Chicken Stock (page 228)

½ cup heavy (whipping) cream

¼ teaspoon freshly ground white pepper (optional)

1. Sauté the onions. Preheat the Instant Pot® by selecting Sauté and adjust to More for high heat. Put the butter in the pot to melt. When it has stopped foaming, add the onion and sprinkle with the salt. Cook, stirring frequently, until the onion pieces separate and soften, 2 to 3 minutes.

2. Prepare the remaining ingredients. Add the wine and cook until it has reduced by about half and the raw alcohol smell is gone, 3 to 5 minutes. Add the asparagus and chicken stock.

3. Pressure cook. Lock the lid into place. Select Manual; adjust the pressure to High and the time to 10 minutes. After cooking, let the pressure release naturally for 10 minutes, then quick release any remaining pressure. Unlock and remove the lid.

4. Finish the soup. Pour about half of the soup into a blender, filling the jar only halfway. Remove the center of the blender lid and hold a dish towel tightly over the hole to allow steam to escape. Purée the soup thoroughly. Pour the soup through a medium-mesh strainer into a bowl, using a rubber spatula to push the soup through the strainer. Discard any pulp and repeat with the remaining soup. Return the soup to the Instant Pot®. Select Sauté and adjust to Normal for medium heat. Add the cream and bring the soup to a simmer. Adjust the seasoning, adding more salt and the white pepper (if using) if desired. Ladle into bowls and serve.

COOKING TIP: When I make this soup with whole bunches of asparagus, I like to cut off the tips (about an inch) and steam them for a garnish before starting the soup. To steam, place the tips in a steamer basket or trivet in the Instant Pot®. Select Steam and set to Low pressure. Lock the lid into place and cook for 1 minute; use quick release and remove the steamer from the pot. Then use the rest of the asparagus stalks to make the soup as directed in the recipe. Garnish the finished soup with the steamed tips.

PER SERVING Calories: 213; Fat: 15g; Sodium: 1518mg; Carbohydrates: 11g; Fiber: 4g; Protein: 5g

CORN ON THE COB
THREE WAYS

When corn is in season, there's no better (or easier) way to eat it than straight off the cob. But easy doesn't mean it has to be boring. As wonderful as plain butter and salt are, I also like to add a few spices for a change. The three combinations below are just a starting point—try your favorite spice blends for an easy, tasty side dish. **SERVES 4**

PREP AND FINISHING
10 minutes

MANUAL
3 minutes
low pressure

RELEASE
Quick

TOTAL TIME
18 MINUTES

30 MIN OR LESS

CORE INGREDIENTS

4 ears corn, shucked and halved crosswise

3 cups hot water

1 teaspoon kosher salt

2 tablespoons unsalted butter

FOR CHIPOTLE-CUMIN CORN

1 teaspoon chipotle purée (see page 22)

1 teaspoon freshly squeezed lime juice

½ teaspoon ground cumin

¼ teaspoon kosher salt

FOR BLACK PEPPER AND PARMESAN CORN

3 tablespoons grated Parmesan or similar cheese

½ teaspoon freshly ground black pepper

¼ teaspoon kosher salt

¼ teaspoon granulated garlic or garlic powder

FOR SPICY CURRIED CORN

1 teaspoon curry powder

½ teaspoon freshly ground black pepper

¼ teaspoon cayenne pepper

¼ teaspoon kosher salt

1. **Pressure cook.** Put the corn in the Instant Pot® and add the water and salt. (Using hot water will shorten the time it takes the cooker to come to pressure.) Lock the lid into place. Select Manual; adjust the pressure to Low and the time to 3 minutes. After cooking, quick release the pressure. Unlock and remove the lid.

2. **Finish the corn.** Use tongs to transfer the corn to a platter. Discard the cooking water and wipe the pot dry. Select Sauté and adjust to More for high heat. Put the butter in the pot, along with the seasonings for the variation you've chosen. When the butter has melted, return the corn to the pot and toss to coat the ears with the seasoned butter. Serve.

INGREDIENT TIP: If you know a little about corn, it's easy to pick out good ears. Both the husks and the silk (if attached) should be supple and fresh, neither dried out nor wet and slimy. The ears should be heavy. Wrap your hand around the corn and give it a squeeze—the kernels inside should be resilient and fill the husks to the top. If there's a big gap under the silk, chances are the corn is beginning to dry out.

PER SERVING Calories: 183; Fat: 8g; Sodium:645mg;Carbohydrates:29g; Fiber: 4g; Protein: 5g

PER SERVING (CHIPOTLE-CUMIN VARIATION) Calories: 185; Fat: 8g; Sodium:825mg;Carbohydrates:29g; Fiber: 4g; Protein: 5g

PER SERVING (BLACK PEPPER AND PARMESAN VARIATION) Calories: 207; Fat: 9g; Sodium:859mg;Carbohydrates:30g; Fiber: 4g; Protein: 7g

PER SERVING (SPICY CURRIED CORN VARIATION) Calories: 186; Fat: 8g; Sodium:793mg;Carbohydrates:30g; Fiber: 5g; Protein: 5g

CAJUN CREAMED CORN

If, like mine, your idea from childhood of creamed corn was the gloppy stuff from a can, you're in for a delightful surprise with this dish, properly known as *maque choux*. Corn, onions, bell peppers, and tomatoes get an extra kick from Cajun spices, and just a touch of cream smoothes out the flavors and texture. And when made with frozen corn in a pressure cooker, it couldn't be quicker or easier. **SERVES 6**

PREP AND FINISHING
10 minutes

MANUAL
3 minutes
high pressure

RELEASE
Quick

TOTAL TIME
20 MINUTES

30 MIN OR LESS

ONE POT

PER SERVING Calories: 118; Fat: 7g; Sodium: 298mg; Carbohydrates: 15g; Fiber: 2g; Protein: 3g

2½ cups frozen corn

½ cup chopped onion (½ medium onion)

⅓ cup chopped red bell pepper (¼ medium pepper)

2 garlic cloves, minced

1 jalapeño, seeded and minced

½ teaspoon Cajun seasoning

½ teaspoon kosher salt, plus more to taste

½ cup Chicken Stock (page 228)

2 tablespoons unsalted butter

¼ cup heavy (whipping) cream

1 very small tomato, seeded and diced (about ¼ cup)

¼ cup thinly sliced scallions

1. **Pressure cook.** In the Instant Pot®, combine the corn, onion, bell pepper, garlic, jalapeño, Cajun seasoning, salt, chicken stock, and butter. Lock the lid into place. Select Manual; adjust the pressure to High and the time to 3 minutes. After cooking, quick release the pressure. Unlock and remove the lid.

2. **Finish the dish.** Select Sauté and adjust to More for high heat. Bring the liquid to a boil and simmer until most of it has evaporated, about 3 minutes. Add the cream and cook until the cream has thickened slightly, 1 to 2 minutes. Add the tomato and scallions and cook just to warm through. Taste and add more salt if needed. Spoon into a serving dish and serve.

INGREDIENT TIP: If you use a commercial Cajun spice blend, check to see if it contains salt. If so, omit the salt at the beginning of cooking and add at the end only if necessary. If you can't find Cajun seasoning, you can make your own easily: Mix ½ teaspoon dried basil, ½ teaspoon dried thyme, ½ teaspoon freshly ground black pepper, ½ teaspoon freshly ground white pepper, and ¼ teaspoon cayenne pepper. This will give you more than this recipe calls for, but you can store leftovers in an airtight container to use in another recipe.

CREOLE CARROTS

Browning the carrots in this recipe gives them a sweetness and complexity that's balanced by the mustard and lemon juice. After browning, a couple of minutes at low pressure results in carrots that are tender but not mushy at all. It's a side dish that will impress any guest—without requiring you to slave over the stove. **SERVES 4**

PREP AND FINISHING
10 minutes

MANUAL
2 minutes
low pressure

RELEASE
Quick

TOTAL TIME
20 MINUTES

30 MIN OR LESS

GRAIN-FREE

ONE POT

PER SERVING Calories: 137; Fat: 10g; Sodium: 479mg; Carbohydrates: 12g; Fiber: 3g; Protein: 2g

3 tablespoons unsalted butter, divided

1 pound carrots, peeled and cut into sticks about 2 inches long and ½ inch on each side

½ teaspoon kosher salt

¼ cup Chicken Stock (page 228)

1 tablespoon freshly squeezed lemon juice

1 tablespoon Creole mustard or other whole-grain mustard

1. **Brown the carrots.** Preheat the Instant Pot® by selecting Sauté and adjust to More for high heat. Put 2 tablespoons of butter in the pot to melt. When the butter has just begun to brown, add the carrots and sprinkle them with the salt. Stir to coat with the butter and then arrange them into a single layer as much as possible. Cook without stirring until the carrots just start to brown, about 2 minutes. Stir to expose another side of the carrots to the heat and repeat until that side begins to brown.

2. **Pressure cook.** Add the stock to the Instant Pot®. Lock the lid into place. Select Manual; adjust the pressure to Low and the time to 2 minutes. After cooking, quick release the pressure. Unlock and remove the lid.

3. **Finish the carrots.** Select Sauté and adjust to More for high heat. Bring the liquid to a boil and cook until almost all the stock has evaporated. Add the lemon juice, mustard, and the remaining 1 tablespoon of butter and stir to coat. Serve.

INGREDIENT TIP: This recipe is also delicious when made with a mix of green beans and carrots.

MASHED SWEET POTATOES
WITH TOASTED ALMONDS

If your sole exposure to sweet potatoes is the super-sweet marshmallow-topped casserole on the holiday table, you owe it to yourself to try them unadorned. Sweet potatoes have a natural affinity for warm spices, and nutmeg is a particularly good match. Toasted almonds add crunch, contrasting nicely with the creamy potatoes. If possible, use a potato ricer, which traps the stringy fibers and results in a smoother texture. For even more flavor, drizzle the finished dish with a little browned butter. **SERVES 4**

PREP AND FINISHING
15 minutes

MANUAL
8 minutes
high pressure

RELEASE
Natural for 10 minutes

TOTAL TIME
40 MINUTES

60 MIN OR LESS

GRAIN-FREE

4 tablespoons unsalted butter, divided

½ cup raw whole almonds, very coarsely chopped

2 large or 4 small sweet potatoes (about 1½ pounds), quartered

1 cup water, for steaming

¼ cup half-and-half

½ teaspoon kosher salt

¼ teaspoon freshly grated nutmeg

1. Toast the almonds. Preheat the Instant Pot® by selecting Sauté and adjust to More for high heat. Put 1 tablespoon of butter in the pot to melt. When the butter has stopped foaming, add the almonds. Cook, stirring, until the almonds are golden brown and fragrant, about 6 minutes. Transfer the almonds to a small bowl and wipe out the pot.

2. Pressure cook the sweet potatoes. Pile the sweet potatoes in a steamer basket and place the basket in the Instant Pot®. Add the water to the pot. Lock the lid into place. Select Manual; adjust the pressure to High and the time to 8 minutes. After cooking, let the pressure release naturally for 10 minutes, then quick release any remaining pressure. Unlock and remove the lid. ➤

3. Mash the potatoes. Remove the steamer from the pot and set the potatoes aside. Pour the water out of the pot and wipe it dry. Select Sauté and adjust to Less for low heat. Pour in the half-and-half and add the remaining 3 tablespoons of butter. Remove the skins from the potatoes. Using a ricer, press the potatoes into the pot and stir to combine with the cream and butter. (If you don't have a ricer, mash the potatoes into the cream and butter with a potato masher or large fork.) Season with the salt.

4. Garnish and serve. Spoon the potatoes into a serving dish. Top with the toasted almonds, sprinkle with the nutmeg, and serve.

PER SERVING Calories: 392; Fat: 20g; Sodium: 251mg; Carbohydrates: 51g; Fiber: 9g; Protein: 6g

EASIEST MASHED POTATOES

I've been using a pressure cooker for mashed potatoes for years, but until recently, I steamed the potatoes and then mashed them with warm milk, cream, and butter. While that method does make excellent potatoes, I've converted to an even easier one. Now I cook the potatoes (and sometimes garlic—see the Tip) with butter and milk, which softens and flavors them. With the right amount of milk, you can mash them right in the pot, resulting in a creamy texture similar to that of whipped potatoes. **SERVES 4**

PREP AND FINISHING
10 minutes

MANUAL
8 minutes
high pressure

RELEASE
Quick

**TOTAL TIME
25 MINUTES**

30 MIN OR LESS

GRAIN-FREE

2 pounds russet potatoes, peeled and cut into 1- to 2-inch chunks

1 teaspoon kosher salt, plus more to taste

1½ cups whole milk

½ cup heavy (whipping) cream

3 tablespoons unsalted butter

¼ teaspoon freshly ground black pepper

1. Pressure cook the potatoes. Put the potatoes in the Instant Pot® and sprinkle them with the salt. Add the milk, cream, and butter. Lock the lid into place. Select Manual; adjust the pressure to High and the time to 8 minutes. After cooking, quick release the pressure. Unlock and remove the lid.

2. Mash the potatoes. Using a potato masher or large fork, mash the potatoes into the milk mixture until smooth and creamy. (Alternatively, you can remove the potatoes with a slotted spoon or skimmer and use a ricer to press the potatoes into the pot, then stir to combine them with the cream and butter.) Season with the pepper and additional salt, if necessary, and serve.

INGREDIENT TIP: For potatoes with a twist, add 6 to 8 whole peeled garlic cloves to the pot before cooking the potatoes. After cooking, add a tablespoon or so of prepared horseradish as you mash the potatoes.

PER SERVING Calories: 340; Fat: 17g; Sodium: 699mg; Carbohydrates: 40g; Fiber: 6g; Protein: 7g

SPAGHETTI SQUASH
WITH FETA, TOMATOES, AND PINE NUTS

I used to think I didn't like spaghetti squash, but that's because I'd only had it served as a substitute for spaghetti noodles with marinara or meat sauce. When in doubt, try another preparation or two before making a final verdict. On its own, dressed simply with butter and Parmesan cheese or more elaborately as in this recipe, spaghetti squash has a nutty sweetness that shines through. The tomatoes and feta balance the sweetness, while toasted pine nuts add crunch. **SERVES 4**

PREP AND FINISHING
10 minutes

STEAM
7 minutes
high pressure

RELEASE
Quick

**TOTAL TIME
25 MINUTES**

30 MIN OR LESS

GRAIN-FREE

1 small spaghetti squash (3 to 4 pounds)

1 cup water, for steaming

¼ cup extra-virgin olive oil

2 tablespoons freshly squeezed lemon juice

¼ teaspoon kosher salt

⅛ teaspoon freshly ground black pepper

1 pint cherry tomatoes, halved

½ cup crumbled feta cheese

3 tablespoons toasted pine nuts

2 tablespoons chopped fresh parsley

1. Prepare the squash. Cut the squash in half lengthwise and scoop out the seeds and pulp.

2. Pressure cook. Place the squash halves, cut-side down, on a trivet. Pour the water into the Instant Pot® and place the trivet inside. Lock the lid into place. Select Steam; adjust the pressure to High and the time to 7 minutes. After cooking, quick release the pressure. Unlock and remove the lid.

3. Make the dressing. While the squash cooks, combine the olive oil, lemon juice, salt, and pepper in a small jar with a tight-fitting lid. Shake until well combined. Set aside.

4. **Finish the dish.** Use tongs to remove the squash halves from the pot. Let them cool slightly, then scrape out the flesh with a fork to form long strands. Transfer the strands to a serving bowl and let cool until just warm. Add the tomatoes and feta cheese. Drizzle with the dressing and toss gently to coat. Top with the pine nuts and parsley and serve.

INGREDIENT TIP: You may be able to find pine nuts already toasted (Trader Joe's sells them), but if not, you can toast them yourself in a small, dry skillet over medium-high heat. Toss or stir until they start to turn golden brown, then remove them from the skillet so they don't continue to cook. Let cool.

PER SERVING Calories: 313; Fat: 22g; Sodium: 370mg; Carbohydrates: 29g; Fiber: 1g; Protein: 6g

SWEET AND SOUR GLAZED BRUSSELS SPROUTS

You probably haven't had Brussels sprouts cooked with apples and a sweet and sour sauce, but it's a perfectly natural pairing if you think of Brussels sprouts as tiny cabbages. I've always loved cabbage prepared that way, so why not sprouts? It turns out to be a delightful combination, not to mention an unexpected and sophisticated presentation. **SERVES 4**

PREP AND FINISHING
20 minutes

MANUAL
1 minute
high pressure

RELEASE
Quick

TOTAL TIME
25 MINUTES

30 MIN OR LESS

GRAIN-FREE

DAIRY-FREE

2 or 3 bacon slices, diced

½ cup chopped onion (½ medium onion)

½ cup chopped peeled apple (½ medium apple)

½ cup apple juice or cider

¼ cup Chicken Stock (page 228)

1 pound Brussels sprouts, trimmed and halved

½ teaspoon kosher salt

2 tablespoons apple cider vinegar

1 tablespoon brown sugar

1. Sauté the bacon, onion, and apple. Preheat the Instant Pot® by selecting Sauté and adjust to Normal for medium heat. Cook the bacon until most of the fat has rendered and the bacon is crisp, about 6 minutes. Use a slotted spoon to remove the bacon, and drain on paper towels, leaving the rendered fat in the pot. Add the onion and apple and cook, stirring frequently, until the onion pieces separate and soften, 2 to 3 minutes.

2. Pressure cook. Add the apple juice and stock to the pot. Put the spouts in a steamer basket and put the basket in the pot. Lock the lid into place. Select Manual; adjust the pressure to High and the time to 1 minute. After cooking, quick release the pressure. Unlock and remove the lid and carefully remove the steamer basket from the pot. Sprinkle the Brussels sprouts with the salt.

3. Make the sauce. Select Sauté and adjust to More for high heat. Bring the liquid to a boil and cook until it has reduced to a glaze (it will be thickened and shiny), about 3 minutes. Stir in the vinegar and brown sugar and bring back to a boil.

4. Finish the dish. Add the Brussels sprouts and stir to coat with the sauce and heat through. Transfer to a bowl, sprinkle with the reserved bacon, and serve.

PER SERVING Calories: 209; Fat: 9g; Sodium: 861mg; Carbohydrates: 22g; Fiber: 5g; Protein: 12g

BROCCOLI AND CAULIFLOWER
WITH CHEESE SAUCE

Broccoli and cauliflower cook beautifully in a pressure cooker as long as you choose a very short cooking time. That allows you to make a quick cheese sauce right in the pot and serve a delectable, sophisticated side dish on a busy weeknight. You'll have no complaints when you serve this dish—and any number of requests for seconds. **SERVES 4**

PREP AND FINISHING
10 minutes

MANUAL
1 minute
low pressure

RELEASE
Quick

**TOTAL TIME
15 MINUTES**

30 MIN OR LESS

2 cups broccoli florets

2 cups cauliflower florets

1 cup water, for steaming

¾ cup evaporated milk

1 tablespoon unsalted butter

2 cups grated sharp Cheddar cheese (about 8 ounces)

1 teaspoon cornstarch

1 teaspoon Dijon-style mustard

1. Pressure cook. Combine the broccoli and cauliflower in a steamer basket. Pour the water into the Instant Pot® and place the steamer basket inside. Lock the lid into place. Select Manual; adjust the pressure to Low and the time to 1 minute. After cooking, quick release the pressure. Unlock and remove the lid.

2. Make the sauce. Use tongs or a potholder to remove the steamer basket. Tent the vegetables loosely with aluminum foil to keep warm. Discard the cooking water in the pot and wipe it dry. Select Sauté and adjust to More for high heat. Pour in the evaporated milk, add the butter, and bring to a simmer. While the milk heats, toss the cheese with the cornstarch in a bowl. Add the cheese a handful at a time, stirring to melt the cheese before adding the next handful. When all the cheese is melted, stir in the mustard.

3. Serve the dish. Transfer the vegetables to a serving bowl, pour the cheese sauce over, and serve.

PER SERVING Calories: 351; Fat: 26g; Sodium: 452mg; Carbohydrates: 12g; Fiber: 3g; Protein: 20g

QUINOA AND CORN SOUP

Adding quinoa to vegetable soup is a delicious and easy way to add protein, but it can be difficult to cook the quinoa correctly. It has a tendency to get gummy when cooked in soup, so I like to cook it separately and add it at the end. This southwestern-inspired soup makes a great lunch, or pair it with quesadillas for a light dinner. **SERVES 4**

PREP AND FINISHING
10 minutes

MANUAL
1 + 3 minutes
high pressure

RELEASE
Natural for
12 + 5 minutes

**TOTAL TIME
30 MINUTES**

30 MIN OR LESS

ONE POT

DAIRY-FREE

1 cup quinoa, rinsed

5½ cups Vegetable Stock (page 229) or Chicken Stock (page 228), divided

1 small onion, diced

2 garlic cloves, minced

1 small red bell pepper, seeded and chopped

1 small green bell pepper, seeded and chopped

1 small russet potato, peeled and cut into ½-inch cubes

3 cups fresh or frozen corn

1 teaspoon ground cumin

1 teaspoon ground ancho chile

1 tablespoon freshly squeezed lime juice

¼ to ½ teaspoon kosher salt

1. Pressure cook the quinoa. Put the quinoa in the Instant Pot®, then pour in 1½ cups of stock. Lock the lid into place. Select Manual; adjust the pressure to High and the time to 1 minute. After cooking, let the pressure release naturally for 12 minutes, then quick release any remaining pressure. Unlock and remove the lid. Spoon the quinoa into a small bowl and fluff it with a fork. Set aside.

2. Pressure cook the soup. Pour the remaining 4 cups of stock into the pot and add the onion, garlic, red and green bell peppers, potato, corn, cumin, and ground chile. Lock the lid into place. Select Manual; adjust the pressure to High and the time to 3 minutes. After cooking, let the pressure release naturally for 5 minutes, then quick release any remaining pressure. Unlock and remove the lid.

3. Finish the soup. Add the quinoa to the soup. Stir in the lime juice and taste, adding salt if necessary. Ladle into soup bowls and serve.

PER SERVING Calories: 332; Fat: 12g; Sodium: 1223mg; Carbohydrates: 64g; Fiber: 9g; Protein: 13g

CREAMY GREEN BEANS AND MUSHROOMS

Think of this dish as a modern, much tastier version of the green bean casserole you may have grown up with—you know, the one with canned fried onion rings and cream of mushroom soup. Even with the green beans, it's the furthest thing from healthy. Here, skip the soup, and combine deliciously browned mushrooms, green beans, and a garlicky cream sauce for the best Thanksgiving side dish ever. **SERVES 6**

PREP AND FINISHING
15 minutes

MANUAL
4 + 2 minutes
low pressure

RELEASE
Quick

TOTAL TIME
30 MINUTES

30 MIN OR LESS

GRAIN-FREE

8 ounces mushrooms

2 tablespoons unsalted butter

½ teaspoon kosher salt, divided

Water, for steaming

1 pound green beans, trimmed and cut into 1-inch lengths

2 garlic cloves, minced

½ cup heavy (whipping) cream

Freshly ground black pepper

1. **Pressure cook the mushrooms.** Cut the stems off the mushrooms, and cut them into quarters if small or eighths if large. Put them in the Instant Pot® with the butter and ¼ teaspoon of salt. Pour in enough water to just barely cover the mushrooms. Lock the lid into place. Select Manual; adjust the pressure to Low and the time to 4 minutes. After cooking, quick release the pressure. Unlock and remove the lid.

2. **Pressure cook the beans.** With the mushrooms still in the pot, put the green beans in a steamer basket and put the basket in the pot. (The mushrooms will be around the feet of the basket.) Lock the lid into place. Select Manual; adjust the pressure to Low and the time to 2 minutes. After cooking, quick release the pressure. Unlock and remove the lid and carefully remove the steamer basket. Sprinkle the beans with the remaining ¼ teaspoon of salt and set aside.

3. **Sauté the mushrooms and garlic.** Select Sauté and adjust to More for high heat. Bring the liquid to a boil and cook until the water has completely evaporated, leaving the butter and mushrooms in the bottom of the pot. Add the garlic to the mushrooms and cook, stirring occasionally, until the mushrooms are browned.

4. **Finish the dish.** Leaving the pot on Sauté, add the cream and cook for a few minutes, just until the cream has thickened. Add the beans and stir to coat and heat through. Taste and adjust the seasoning, adding the remaining salt and some black pepper. Spoon into a serving dish and serve.

SERVING TIP: If you want to make this dish more like the traditional green bean casserole (and don't need it to be grain-free), spoon the beans into a heat-proof dish. Top the beans with canned onion rings or buttered panko bread crumbs and place under a preheated broiler until the top is browned.

PER SERVING Calories: 101; Fat: 8g; Sodium: 232mg; Carbohydrates: 7g; Fiber: 3g; Protein: 3g

BRAISED GREEN BEANS
WITH BACON

I grew up eating braised green beans with onions and bacon. Looking back on it, I see now that the beans were cooked long past their prime, but that's what cooks used to do—they sacrificed texture for flavor. But you don't have to make that compromise. When pressure cooked, the beans absorb the flavor of the onions and bacon while retaining their color and texture. **SERVES 4**

PREP AND FINISHING
15 minutes

STEAM
3 minutes
low pressure

RELEASE
Quick

**TOTAL TIME
20 MINUTES**

30 MIN OR LESS

GRAIN-FREE

DAIRY-FREE

4 bacon slices, chopped

1 small onion, chopped

½ teaspoon kosher salt, divided

1 pound green beans, trimmed and cut into 1½-inch lengths

⅓ cup Chicken Stock (page 228) or Vegetable Stock (page 229)

1. Sauté the bacon and onions. Preheat the Instant Pot® by selecting Sauté and adjust to Normal for medium heat. Cook the bacon until most of the fat has rendered and the bacon is crisp, about 6 minutes. Use a slotted spoon to remove the bacon, and drain on paper towels, leaving the rendered fat in the pot. Add the onion and sprinkle with ¼ teaspoon of salt. Cook, stirring frequently, until the onion pieces separate and soften, 2 to 3 minutes.

2. Pressure cook. Add the beans to the pressure cooker and sprinkle with the remaining ¼ teaspoon of salt. Stir to coat the beans with the onion and fat. Add the stock to the pot. Lock the lid into place. Select Steam; adjust the pressure to Low and the time to 3 minutes. After cooking, quick release the pressure. Unlock and remove the lid.

3. Finish the dish. Spoon the beans into a serving dish, drizzling them with a little of the braising liquid. Top with the reserved bacon and serve.

PER SERVING Calories: 200; Fat: 12g; Sodium: 1016mg; Carbohydrates: 11g; Fiber: 5g; Protein: 13g

PICKLED BEETS

My father loved pickled beets, so one year for his birthday, I made a batch of them following a recipe from the book *Quick Pickles* by Chris Schlesinger, John Willoughby, and Dan George. With orange juice, red wine, spices, and horse-radish, they were (I thought) delicious. Dad was very polite, but I could tell he preferred the plainer version he was used to. Live and learn, as they say—but it meant there were more for me! This is my version of that recipe, which goes much faster now that I've learned how to cook beets in a pressure cooker. **SERVES 6**

PREP AND FINISHING
15 minutes

MANUAL
10 minutes
high pressure

RELEASE
Quick

TOTAL TIME
30 MINUTES, PLUS
2 HOURS TO CHILL

GRAIN-FREE

DAIRY-FREE

2 pounds medium beets (about 2 inches across), trimmed but not peeled

1 cup water, for steaming

1 medium orange

¾ cup red wine vinegar

½ cup dry red wine

⅓ cup sugar

1 teaspoon whole cloves

1 teaspoon whole allspice berries

¼ teaspoon whole black peppercorns

1 tablespoon prepared horseradish

1. **Pressure cook the beets.** Pile the beets in a steamer basket and place the basket in the Instant Pot®. Add the water to the pot. Lock the lid into place. Select Manual; adjust the pressure to High and the time to 10 minutes. After cooking, quick release the pressure. Unlock and remove the lid and carefully remove the steamer basket from the pot. As soon as the beets are cool enough to handle, remove and discard the skin and cut them into ¼-inch slices, then cut the slices in half to form half-moons. Set aside in a medium bowl or in several mason jars.

2. Make the pickling liquid. Pour the water out of the pot. Peel the zest from the orange (a serrated peeler is great for this) into the pot, then juice the orange and add the juice to the pot. Add the vinegar, wine, sugar, cloves, allspice berries, and peppercorns to the pot. Select Sauté and adjust to More for high heat. Bring the liquid to a boil and cook until the sugar has dissolved, 2 to 3 minutes. Turn off the heat and stir in the horseradish.

3. Finish the beets. Pour the hot pickling liquid over the beets. Let cool to room temperature, then refrigerate. The beets can be eaten after a couple of hours, but for best results, cover tightly and refrigerate for 8 hours or overnight. The beets will keep in an airtight container in the refrigerator for several weeks.

PER SERVING Calories: 146; Fat: 0g; Sodium: 127mg; Carbohydrates: 31g; Fiber: 4g; Protein: 3g

BETTER THAN MOM'S POTATO SALAD

Don't get me wrong—my mother made good potato salad. I started out following her recipe, but over the years, I've made a few changes. First, she used russet potatoes, which tend to fall apart in a salad. I use red potatoes, which hold their shape better. She used dill pickles; I use capers, which are much more complex in flavor. And I add a lot of fresh herbs. The combination of mayonnaise, sour cream, and yogurt might seem fussy, but they contribute different flavors and textures to the dressing. Once you taste this, I think you'll agree it's worth the extra effort! **SERVES 4**

PREP AND FINISHING
15 minutes

STEAM
4 minutes
high pressure

RELEASE
Quick

TOTAL TIME
25 MINUTES

30 MIN OR LESS

GRAIN-FREE

1 pound small red potatoes (about 2 inches in diameter), quartered

2 large eggs, in their shells

1 cup water, for steaming

1 tablespoon red or white wine vinegar

¾ teaspoon kosher salt, divided

¼ cup mayonnaise, plus more to taste

2 tablespoons sour cream

2 tablespoons plain Yogurt (page 230)

¼ teaspoon freshly ground black pepper

¼ teaspoon celery seed

1 large celery stalk, sliced thin (about ⅔ cup)

½ cup sliced scallions (1 to 2 scallions)

2 tablespoons chopped fresh dill

2 tablespoons chopped fresh parsley

1 tablespoon drained capers

1. Make an ice bath. Fill a small bowl about halfway with cold water. Add a couple of handfuls of ice cubes. Set aside.

2. Pressure cook. Place the potato quarters and eggs in a steamer basket. Pour the water into the Instant Pot® and place the steamer basket inside. Lock the lid into place. Select Steam; adjust the pressure to High and the time to 4 minutes. After cooking, quick release the pressure. Unlock and remove the lid.

3. Prepare the eggs and potatoes. Use tongs to transfer the eggs to the ice bath. Remove the steamer basket with the potatoes and set it over a medium bowl. Sprinkle the potatoes with the vinegar and ½ teaspoon of salt. Let the potatoes cool while you make the dressing.

4. Make the dressing. In a small bowl, whisk together the mayonnaise, sour cream, yogurt, remaining ¼ teaspoon of salt, black pepper, and celery seed. Set aside.

5. Finish the salad. Transfer the potatoes to a large bowl and use a large fork or spoon to break up the potatoes into bite-size pieces. Add the celery, scallions, dill, parsley, and capers to the potatoes. Pour the dressing over the salad and stir gently to coat, adding more mayonnaise if necessary to coat thoroughly. When the eggs are cold, peel and dice them, then add them to the salad and toss gently. Serve.

SERVING TIP: For a classic presentation, slice the eggs rather than dicing them and arrange them on top of the salad. Sprinkle with paprika.

PER SERVING Calories: 197; Fat: 9g; Sodium: 662mg; Carbohydrates: 25g; Fiber: 4g; Protein: 6g

CLASSIC THANKSGIVING STUFFING

I have to admit, I'm one of those people who want their stuffing to be, well, stuffing. That is, I always think it's better cooked in the bird. On the other hand, it's much easier to cook a turkey properly if it's not stuffed. What to do? Using the pressure cooker instead of baking the stuffing results in a texture that's extra moist and tender, almost as if it came out of the bird itself. **SERVES 6**

PREP AND FINISHING
15 minutes

MANUAL
12 minutes
high pressure

RELEASE
Natural for 10 minutes

**TOTAL TIME
35 MINUTES**

60 MIN OR LESS

1 tablespoon unsalted butter

4 ounces breakfast sausage, removed from its casings

1 cup chopped onion

2 celery stalks, diced (about 1 cup)

4 cups (1-inch) stale bread cubes (3 to 4 bread slices)

1 teaspoon crumbled dried sage

½ teaspoon poultry seasoning

½ teaspoon kosher salt

¼ teaspoon freshly ground black pepper

1 large egg

1¼ cups Chicken Stock (page 228)

1 cup water, for steaming

1. Brown the sausage and vegetables. Preheat the Instant Pot® by selecting Sauté and adjust to Normal for medium heat. Put the butter in the pot to melt. When it has stopped foaming, add the sausage, breaking it up with a spatula or wooden spoon into small pieces. Cook, stirring frequently, until the sausage pieces are browned. Don't worry if they aren't cooked through all the way. Add the onion and celery and cook, stirring, until the vegetables have softened, about 3 minutes. Transfer the sausage and vegetables to a large bowl and rinse out the pot.

2. Prepare the stuffing. Add the bread cubes, sage, poultry seasoning, salt, and black pepper to the bowl with the sausage and vegetables. Toss gently to combine. In a small bowl, whisk together the egg and chicken stock. Pour over the bread mixture and toss to combine. Transfer the stuffing to a 1-quart baking dish and cover loosely with aluminum foil.

3. Pressure cook. Pour the water into the Instant Pot®. Place a trivet with handles in the pot and place the baking dish on top. If your trivet doesn't have handles, use a foil sling (see page 16) to make removing the dish easier. Lock the lid into place. Select Manual; adjust the pressure to High and the time to 12 minutes. After cooking, naturally release the pressure for 10 minutes, then quick release any remaining pressure. Unlock and remove the lid.

4. Finish the stuffing. Carefully remove the dish from the pot and serve the stuffing.

COOKING TIP: If you like a crisp top to your stuffing, bake the dish in a preheated 375°F oven until browned on top, about 10 minutes.

PER SERVING Calories: 119; Fat: 8g; Sodium: 565mg; Carbohydrates: 5g; Fiber: 1g; Protein: 6g

HUMMUS WITH AVOCADO (PAGE 82)

CHAPTER 4
BEANS & GRAINS

Once you start cooking beans and grains in your Instant Pot®, you'll never go back to stove top or oven cooking for them. It's true that most of the bean recipes here require presoaking, but that just takes a little forethought and 5 minutes of your time. You can start soaking beans up to 24 hours in advance, or as little as 8 hours before you cook. Keep in mind that cooking beans and most grains in a pressure cooker produces a bit of foaming, which in large batches can interfere with the pressure gauge. Smaller batches are better, and a bit of oil or butter in the pot helps minimize the foaming.

COWBOY PINTO BEANS

A little bit smoky, a little bit spicy, these savory beans are the perfect side dish for all kinds of meals—think burgers and hot dogs on the grill, Carnitas (page 176), or Chili con Carne (page 190). The bacon, onions, and two kinds of chiles provide a complex flavor that will make you think they've been simmering all day long. But once the beans have soaked overnight, they're done in less than an hour. **SERVES 4**

PREP AND FINISHING
15 minutes

MANUAL
15 minutes
high pressure

RELEASE
Natural for 10 minutes

**TOTAL TIME
45 MINUTES,
PLUS OVERNIGHT
TO SOAK**

GRAIN-FREE

DAIRY-FREE

1 tablespoon plus ½ teaspoon kosher salt, divided

1 quart water

8 ounces dried pinto beans

2 or 3 bacon slices, chopped

1 large onion, chopped (about 1½ cups)

2 garlic cloves, minced

2 cups Chicken Stock (page 228)

¼ cup Ancho Chile Sauce (page 239)

½ teaspoon chipotle purée (optional; see page 22)

1 small tomato, seeded and diced

1 tablespoon chopped fresh cilantro

1. Soak the beans. In a large bowl, dissolve 1 tablespoon of salt in the water. Add the pinto beans and soak at room temperature for 8 to 24 hours. Drain and rinse.

2. Sauté the bacon and onions. Preheat the Instant Pot® by selecting Sauté and adjust to Normal for medium heat. Cook the bacon until most of the fat has rendered and the bacon is crisp, about 6 minutes. Use a slotted spoon to remove the bacon, and drain on paper towels, leaving the rendered fat in the pot. Add the onion and garlic and sprinkle with ¼ teaspoon of salt. Cook, stirring, until the onion pieces separate and soften, 2 to 3 minutes.

3. **Pressure cook.** Add the drained pinto beans, the remaining ¼ teaspoon of salt, the stock, the ancho chile sauce, and the chipotle purée (if using). Lock the lid into place. Select Manual; adjust the pressure to High and the time to 15 minutes. After cooking, naturally release the pressure for 10 minutes, then quick release any remaining pressure. Unlock and remove the lid.

4. **Finish the beans.** Stir in the tomato and cilantro. Taste the beans and adjust the seasoning if needed. If the beans are too soupy, select Sauté and adjust to Normal for medium heat. Simmer until the beans thicken. Transfer to a serving bowl and serve.

PER SERVING Calories: 337; Fat: 10g; Sodium: 1173mg; Carbohydrates: 41g; Fiber: 10g; Protein: 21g

REFRIED BLACK BEANS

While pinto beans are the usual choice for refritos, black beans are also great in this classic Mexican dish. Refritos is better translated as "super-fried beans" than "refried beans," which to me always sounds like a sad leftover dish. Instead, in Mexico, they're the special way to serve beans, emulsified and enriched with pork fat. Here I spice them up with a hint of chipotle and green chiles. Super-fried, indeed! **SERVES 4**

PREP AND FINISHING
15 minutes

MANUAL
30 minutes
high pressure

RELEASE
Natural for 15 minutes

TOTAL TIME
1 HOUR 5 MINUTES

GRAIN-FREE

DAIRY-FREE

8 ounces dried black beans

1 quart water

1 teaspoon kosher salt

1 bacon slice

1 medium onion, peeled and halved, divided

¼ cup lard, bacon fat, or extra-virgin olive oil

2 garlic cloves, lightly smashed

½ teaspoon chipotle purée (see page 22)

¼ cup canned diced green chiles, drained

1. Pressure cook the beans. Put the beans in the Instant Pot® and add the water, salt, bacon, and half of the onion. Lock the lid into place. Select Manual; adjust the pressure to High and the time to 30 minutes. After cooking, naturally release the pressure for 15 minutes, then quick release any remaining pressure. Unlock and remove the lid. The beans should be starting to fall apart.

2. Prep the beans. Place a strainer or colander over a bowl and pour the beans into the strainer, reserving the cooking liquid in the bowl. Remove the onion and bacon (they may have partially dissolved) and discard. Wipe out the pot.

3. **Make the refritos.** Cut the remaining onion half into quarters. Preheat the Instant Pot® by selecting Sauté and adjust to More for high heat. Heat the lard in the pot. When the fat just starts to smoke, add the onion quarters and smashed garlic cloves and cook, turning occasionally, until the vegetables are quite browned, 4 to 5 minutes. Remove and discard them, leaving the fat in the pot. Add the beans and ½ cup of the reserved bean liquid and mash the beans with a potato masher or the back of a fork. Add more liquid if necessary to make a fairly smooth purée. Stir in the chipotle purée and green chiles. Transfer to a serving bowl and serve.

PER SERVING Calories: 358; Fat: 16g; Sodium: 809mg; Carbohydrates: 40g; Fiber: 9g; Protein: 15g

HUMMUS
WITH AVOCADO

I was skeptical when I read about hummus with avocado. I like the classic version so well that I wasn't eager to start tinkering with it. But on reflection, it occurred to me that if you take the tahini out of hummus, the avocado can stand in with its own nutty flavor and rich texture. When I tried it, I was sold. Give it a try and you might be, too. **SERVES 4**

PREP AND FINISHING
15 minutes

MANUAL
5 minutes
high pressure

RELEASE
Natural for 20 minutes

**TOTAL TIME
45 MINUTES,
PLUS OVERNIGHT
TO SOAK**

GRAIN-FREE

DAIRY-FREE

1 tablespoon plus 2 teaspoons kosher salt, divided

2 quarts water, divided

8 ounces dried chickpeas

4 to 5 tablespoons plus 1 teaspoon extra-virgin olive oil, divided

2 tablespoons freshly squeezed lemon juice, plus more to taste

1 large garlic clove, minced

3 tablespoons ice water

1 small avocado, peeled, pitted, and diced

1 tablespoon chopped fresh parsley

2 teaspoons za'atar (optional)

1. Soak the chickpeas. In a large bowl, dissolve 1 tablespoon of salt in 1 quart of water. Add the chickpeas and soak at room temperature for 8 to 24 hours. Drain and rinse.

2. Pressure cook the chickpeas. Put the chickpeas in the Instant Pot® and add the remaining 1 quart of water, the remaining 2 teaspoons of salt, and 1 teaspoon of olive oil. Lock the lid into place. Select Manual; adjust the pressure to High and the time to 5 minutes. After cooking, naturally release the pressure for 20 minutes, then quick release any remaining pressure. Unlock and remove the lid.

3. Make the hummus. Drain the chickpeas in a strainer or colander. Remove any loose skins (this makes the hummus smoother) and transfer the chickpeas to the bowl of a food processor. Add 3 tablespoons of olive oil, the lemon juice, and garlic and pulse to form a coarse paste. Scrape down the sides of the bowl with a spatula and then process until the paste smoothes out. With the motor running, slowly drizzle in the ice water through the feed tube until the hummus is smooth. Add the avocado and pulse two or three times. You want the avocado to remain mostly in chunks. Taste and add more lemon juice and salt if needed.

4. Serve the hummus. Scoop the hummus into a bowl. Drizzle with the remaining 1 to 2 tablespoons of olive oil and sprinkle with the parsley and za'atar (if using) and serve.

PER SERVING Calories: 472; Fat: 32g; Sodium: 1182mg; Carbohydrates: 39g; Fiber: 13g; Protein: 12g

BLACK-EYED PEAS AND GREENS

This delicious southern favorite is traditionally an all-day affair—no wonder it's ordinarily reserved for New Year's Day! With a pressure cooker, the active time is cut to a couple of hours with no loss of flavor, so you can make it more than once a year. Smoked pork hocks can be substituted for the smoked turkey parts (and, in fact, are more traditional in this dish). They tend to be fattier, so you may have to skim the broth before using. **SERVES 4**

PREP AND FINISHING
15 minutes

MANUAL
35 + 18 minutes
high pressure

RELEASE
Natural for
10 + 5 minutes

**TOTAL TIME
1 HOUR
30 MINUTES,
PLUS OVERNIGHT
TO SOAK**

ONE POT

GRAIN-FREE

DAIRY-FREE

1 tablespoon kosher salt, plus more for seasoning

2 quarts water, divided

8 ounces dried black-eyed peas

1 or 2 smoked turkey wings or legs

1 small onion, peeled and halved

1 bay leaf

½ teaspoon dried thyme

½ teaspoon freshly ground black pepper, plus more for seasoning

¼ teaspoon red pepper flakes

8 cups chopped collard greens

1 tablespoon red wine vinegar

1. **Soak the beans.** In a large bowl, dissolve the salt in 1 quart of water. Add the black-eyed peas and soak at room temperature for 8 to 24 hours. Drain and rinse.

2. **Pressure cook the broth.** Put the turkey wing(s) in the Instant Pot® and add the remaining 1 quart of water. Lock the lid into place. Select Manual (or Soup); adjust the pressure to High and the time to 35 minutes. After cooking, naturally release the pressure for 10 minutes, then quick release any remaining pressure. Unlock and remove the lid.

3. **Remove the wing(s) and broth.** Remove the wing(s) from the pressure cooker and let cool. Pour the cooking liquid into a bowl or large container and reserve. Shred the meat and set aside. (If you like, you can do steps 2 and 3 while the beans are soaking. Refrigerate the broth and meat until ready to use.)

4. Pressure cook the beans and greens. Put the drained black-eyed peas in the Instant Pot®, along with the onion halves, bay leaf, thyme, black pepper, and red pepper flakes. Put the greens on top of the beans and pour in the reserved turkey cooking liquid. Lock the lid into place. Select Manual; adjust the pressure to High and the time to 18 minutes. After cooking, naturally release the pressure for 5 minutes, then quick release any remaining pressure.

5. Finish the dish. Unlock and remove the lid. Remove the bay leaf and onion halves, then stir in the reserved meat and the vinegar. Let simmer for a minute to warm the meat through. Taste and adjust the seasoning with more salt and black pepper if needed. If the peas or greens aren't done to your liking, select Sauté and simmer for a few minutes. Ladle into bowls and serve.

INGREDIENT TIP: You can save even more time by buying a bag of washed, chopped collard greens. If you buy a bunch, however, make sure to wash the greens thoroughly; they can hide a lot of dirt. Remove the ribs and cut the leaves into ribbons.

PER SERVING Calories: 152; Fat: 3g; Sodium: 296mg; Carbohydrates: 23g; Fiber: 8g; Protein: 13g

ITALIAN CHICKPEA STEW
WITH PESTO

Chickpeas are the basis for this savory Italian stew, which gets an extra kick from a spoonful of intensely flavored pesto at serving time. This recipe calls for making the pesto from scratch because I don't think store-bought pesto can match the flavor of homemade. But premade pesto is a timesaver—not to mention that it makes this recipe a one-pot meal. **SERVES 4**

PREP AND FINISHING
15 minutes

MANUAL
10 minutes
high pressure

RELEASE
Natural for 10 minutes

**TOTAL TIME
40 MINUTES,
PLUS OVERNIGHT
TO SOAK**

GRAIN-FREE

FOR THE PESTO

1½ packed cups fresh basil leaves (about ¾ ounce)

¼ cup extra-virgin olive oil, plus additional if needed

¼ cup grated Parmesan cheese (about 1 ounce)

1 garlic clove, minced

1 tablespoon toasted pine nuts

FOR THE CHICKPEAS

1 tablespoon plus ½ teaspoon kosher salt, divided

1 quart water

12 ounces dried chickpeas

2 tablespoons extra-virgin olive oil

1 small onion, chopped (about ¾ cup)

2 medium carrots, peeled and chopped (about ¾ cup)

1 (14-ounce) can diced tomatoes, undrained

4 cups Chicken Stock (page 228)

¼ cup grated Parmesan or similar cheese

1. Make the pesto. Combine the basil, oil, cheese, garlic, and pine nuts in a small food processor or blender. Pulse until a coarse paste forms, adding a tablespoon or two of water or more olive oil, if necessary to get a loose-enough consistency. Set aside ⅓ cup of pesto for this recipe; the remainder can be refrigerated in an airtight container for a week or so, or frozen for several months.

2. Soak the chickpeas. In a large bowl, dissolve 1 tablespoon of kosher salt in the water. Add the chickpeas and soak at room temperature for 8 to 24 hours. Drain and rinse. ➤

3. Sauté the onions. Preheat the Instant Pot® by selecting Sauté and adjust to More for high heat. Add the olive oil and heat until it shimmers. Add the onion and sprinkle with ¼ teaspoon of salt. Cook, stirring frequently, until the onion pieces separate and soften, 2 to 3 minutes.

4. Pressure cook. Add the drained chickpeas, carrots, tomatoes with their juice, stock, and remaining ¼ teaspoon of salt. Lock the lid into place. Select Manual; adjust the pressure to High and the time to 10 minutes. After cooking, naturally release the pressure for 10 minutes, then quick release any remaining pressure. Unlock and remove the lid.

5. Serve the chickpeas. Ladle the chickpeas into bowls and top each with a spoonful of pesto. Sprinkle with the cheese and serve.

PER SERVING Calories: 592; Fat: 30g; Sodium: 1234mg; Carbohydrates: 63g; Fiber: 18g; Protein: 24g

WHITE BEAN SOUP
WITH CHARD

Creamy beans and chard are a common combination in Italian cuisine, either with or without meat. They're sometimes served over pasta or polenta or, as in this dish, as a delicious, hearty soup. **SERVES 4**

PREP AND FINISHING
15 minutes

MANUAL
15 minutes
high pressure

RELEASE
Natural for 10 minutes

**TOTAL TIME
45 MINUTES,
PLUS OVERNIGHT
TO SOAK**

ONE POT

GRAIN-FREE

PER SERVING Calories: 457; Fat: 13g; Sodium: 1422mg; Carbohydrates: 60g; Fiber: 24g; Protein: 30g

1 tablespoon plus ½ teaspoon kosher salt, divided

1 quart water

12 ounces dried cannellini beans

2 tablespoons extra-virgin olive oil

1 medium onion, chopped (about 1 cup)

1 large carrot, peeled and chopped (about ⅔ cup)

2 garlic cloves, minced

1 cup diced cooked ham

2½ cups Chicken Stock (page 228)

1 small bunch chard, stems removed and leaves cut into 1-inch ribbons

¼ cup grated Parmesan or similar cheese

1 tablespoon chopped fresh parsley

1. Soak the beans. In a large bowl, dissolve 1 tablespoon of kosher salt in the water. Add the beans and soak at room temperature for 8 to 24 hours. Drain and rinse.

2. Sauté the aromatics. Preheat the Instant Pot® by selecting Sauté and adjust to Normal for medium heat. Heat the olive oil until it shimmers. Add the onion and carrot and sprinkle with ¼ teaspoon of salt. Cook, stirring frequently, until the onion pieces separate and soften, 2 to 3 minutes. Add the garlic and cook until fragrant, about another 1 minute.

3. Pressure cook. Add the drained beans to the pot, along with the ham, stock, and remaining ¼ teaspoon of salt. Lock the lid into place. Select Manual; adjust the pressure to High and the time to 15 minutes. After cooking, naturally release the pressure for 10 minutes, then quick release any remaining pressure. Unlock and remove the lid.

4. Finish the beans. Select Sauté and adjust to Normal for medium heat. Stir in the chard. Bring to a simmer and cook until the chard is tender, about 5 minutes. Taste the beans and season with more salt if needed. Ladle the beans into bowls, sprinkle with the cheese and parsley, and serve.

LENTILS
WITH SHORT RIBS

I first had this dish at the home of our dear, now-departed friend Steven Shaw. It was one of his signature dishes, and it is absolutely delicious—way more than the sum of its parts. I later asked him how he made it, and it turned out that he took a couple of days, working in stages. I was more impatient, so I came up with a streamlined version. His was better, but mine is pretty good, if I do say so myself. **SERVES 4**

PREP AND FINISHING
20 minutes

MANUAL
40 + 15 minutes
high pressure

RELEASE
Natural for
10 + 10 minutes

**TOTAL TIME
1 HOUR 45 MINUTES**

ONE POT

GRAIN-FREE

DAIRY-FREE

1½ pounds (2-inch) bone-in short ribs

1¾ teaspoons kosher salt, divided

4 tablespoons extra-virgin olive oil, divided, plus additional if needed

1 medium onion, diced, divided

1 cup dry sherry, divided

2 cups low-sodium beef broth

1 celery stalk, diced

1 carrot, peeled and diced

2 garlic cloves, minced

12 ounces green or brown lentils, rinsed

1. Sear the ribs. Season the short ribs on all sides with 1 teaspoon of salt. Preheat the Instant Pot® by selecting Sauté and adjust to More for high heat. Heat 2 tablespoons of oil until it shimmers. Add the short ribs in a single layer without crowding them. Brown the ribs on all sides, then remove and set aside, changing the cooker to medium heat or the Brown setting.

2. Cook the onions. Add another coat of oil if the pot is dry and heat it until shimmering. Add half of the diced onion. Sprinkle with ¼ teaspoon of salt and stir until the onion pieces just start to brown, 3 to 4 minutes. Add ½ cup of sherry and cook until the liquid has reduced by about half, 2 to 3 minutes. Scrape the bottom of the pot to get up any browned bits.

3. **Pressure cook the ribs.** Return the short ribs to the pot and add the broth. Lock the lid into place. Select Manual; adjust the pressure to High and the time to 40 minutes. After cooking, naturally release the pressure for 10 minutes, then quick release any remaining pressure. Unlock and remove the lid and transfer the ribs to a plate to cool. When they can be handled, remove the meat from the bones and shred it, discarding the fat and connective tissue. Set aside.

4. **Prepare the cooking liquid.** Strain the cooking liquid into a fat separator and set aside. (If you don't have a fat separator, let the sauce sit for a few minutes, then spoon or blot off any excess fat from the top of the sauce.) Discard the onion. Wipe out the pot.

5. **Cook the vegetables for the lentils.** Preheat the pot by selecting Sauté and adjust to More for high heat. Add the remaining 2 tablespoons of oil to the pot and heat until it shimmers. Add the remaining onion, the celery, the carrot, and the garlic and cook, stirring frequently, until the vegetables start to soften, 2 to 3 minutes. Pour in the remaining ½ cup of sherry and cook until the raw alcohol smell is gone, 1 to 2 minutes more.

6. **Pressure cook the lentils.** Add the lentils, the remaining ½ teaspoon of salt, and the defatted cooking liquid. Lock the lid into place. Select Manual; adjust the pressure to High and the time to 15 minutes. After cooking, naturally release the pressure for 10 minutes, then quick release any remaining pressure. Unlock and remove the lid.

7. **Finish the dish.** Taste and adjust the seasoning if needed. Stir in the reserved short rib meat. Let sit for a few minutes to warm the meat through, then serve.

PER SERVING Calories: 846; Fat: 31g; Sodium: 1536mg; Carbohydrates: 58g; Fiber: 27g; Protein: 73g

RICE PILAF
THREE WAYS

Many culinary traditions have some version of rice pilaf—rice sautéed with aromatic vegetables and cooked in savory stock. It's such an easy recipe to adapt that we have our beginning cooking students devise their own pilafs as an exercise in improvisation. These are three classic flavor combinations, but feel free to make any adjustments or changes that you like. Add any raw or sturdy vegetables at the beginning with the onions, and any tender cooked vegetables or fresh herbs at the end. **SERVES 6**

PREP AND FINISHING
15 minutes

MANUAL
8 minutes
high pressure

RELEASE
Quick

TOTAL TIME
30 MINUTES

30 MIN OR LESS

CORE INGREDIENTS

2 tablespoons unsalted butter

½ cup chopped onion

1 cup long-grain white rice

1¼ cups Chicken Stock (page 228) or Vegetable Stock (page 229)

½ teaspoon kosher salt

FOR ALMOND-PARMESAN PILAF

1 garlic clove, minced

¼ cup grated Parmesan or similar cheese

½ cup toasted slivered almonds

FOR GREEK LEMON PILAF

½ cup canned or frozen artichoke hearts, thawed and coarsely chopped

2 tablespoons chopped fresh oregano

1 teaspoon grated lemon zest

2 teaspoons freshly squeezed lemon juice

FOR PEAS AND PARSLEY PILAF

⅓ cup frozen green peas, thawed

2 tablespoons chopped fresh parsley

1. **Sauté the onion and rice.** Preheat the Instant Pot® by selecting Sauté and adjust to Normal for medium heat. Put the butter in the pot to melt. When it has stopped foaming, add the onion.

For Almond-Parmesan Pilaf: Add the garlic.

For all variations: Cook, stirring frequently, until the onion pieces separate and soften, 2 to 3 minutes. Add the rice and stir to coat in the butter, cooking for about 1 minute.

2. Pressure cook. Add the stock and salt.

For Greek Lemon Pilaf: Add the artichoke hearts.

For all variations: Lock the lid into place. Select Manual; adjust the pressure to High and the time to 8 minutes. After cooking, quick release the pressure. Unlock and remove the lid.

3. Finish the pilaf. Add the remaining ingredients, depending on which variation you chose, and stir gently to combine. Put the lid on the pot but do not lock it into place. Let the pilaf sit until the rice is completely cooked and the remaining ingredients are warmed through, 5 to 6 minutes. Fluff with a fork and serve.

PER SERVING Calories: 152; Fat: 4g; Sodium: 382mg; Carbohydrates: 26g; Fiber: 1g; Protein: 3g

PER SERVING (ALMOND-PARMESAN PILAF VARIATION) Calories: 214; Fat: 9g; Sodium: 426mg; Carbohydrates: 28g; Fiber: 2g; Protein: 6g

PER SERVING (GREEK LEMON PILAF VARIATION) Calories: 163; Fat: 4g; Sodium: 394mg; Carbohydrates: 28g; Fiber: 2g; Protein: 3g

PER SERVING (PEAS AND PARSLEY PILAF VARIATION) Calories: 159; Fat: 4g; Sodium: 383mg; Carbohydrates: 27g; Fiber: 1g; Protein: 3g

BARLEY SALAD
WITH RED CABBAGE AND FETA

Cabbage and walnuts give flavor and crunch to chewy barley in this unusual yet delicious salad. Salting the cabbage softens it without making it limp, and also keeps it from leaching water into the salad as it sits. It makes a wonderful side dish for grilled chicken or pork, or it can stand alone as a light lunch. **SERVES 6**

PREP AND FINISHING
20 minutes

MANUAL
10 minutes
high pressure

RELEASE
Natural for 15 minutes

**TOTAL TIME
50 MINUTES**

60 MIN OR LESS

ONE POT

1 cup pearl barley

2½ cups Vegetable Stock (page 229)

¼ cup plus 2 teaspoons extra-virgin olive oil, divided

2 teaspoons kosher salt, divided, plus more to taste

2 cups shredded red cabbage

⅔ cup toasted walnut halves and pieces

2 tablespoons freshly squeezed lemon juice

1 tablespoon chopped fresh parsley

½ cup crumbled feta cheese

1. Pressure cook the barley. Pour the barley into the Instant Pot®. Add the stock, 2 teaspoons of olive oil, and ½ teaspoon of salt. Lock the lid into place. Select Manual; adjust the pressure to High and the time to 10 minutes. After cooking, naturally release the pressure for 15 minutes, then quick release any remaining pressure. Unlock and remove the lid. Taste the barley to make sure it's done; if not, place the lid back on, unlocked, and let the barley steam for a few more minutes.

2. Prepare the cabbage. While the barley cooks, put the cabbage in a salad spinner or colander and sprinkle with the remaining 1½ teaspoons of salt. Toss to combine. Let the cabbage sit for 10 to 15 minutes, then rinse thoroughly and spin or pat dry.

3. Make the salad. Combine the barley, cabbage, and walnuts in a large bowl. Drizzle with the remaining ¼ cup of olive oil and the lemon juice and toss gently to coat with the dressing. Taste and add more salt if necessary. Top with the parsley and feta cheese and serve.

PER SERVING Calories: 350; Fat: 24g; Sodium: 1242mg; Carbohydrates: 26g; Fiber: 7g; Protein: 11g

QUINOA SALAD
WITH BEETS AND SWEET POTATOES

The first time I ever had quinoa, it was in a salad. I'd never even heard of quinoa at the time, but salad remains my favorite way to serve it. Combining it with beets and sweet potatoes is not only tasty, but it also makes a nutritionally balanced and filling vegetarian meal. **SERVES 6**

PREP AND FINISHING
10 minutes

MANUAL
1 + 4 minutes
high pressure

RELEASE
Natural for
12 + 5 minutes

**TOTAL TIME
35 MINUTES**

60 MIN OR LESS

ONE POT

DAIRY-FREE

PER SERVING Calories: 213;
Fat: 11g; Sodium: 214mg;
Carbohydrates: 25g;
Fiber: 3g; Protein: 6g

1 cup quinoa, rinsed

1½ cups Vegetable Stock (page 229) or water

¼ teaspoon kosher salt (if using water), plus more to taste

1 cup water, for steaming

1 large beet, peeled and cut into ¾-inch cubes

1 medium sweet potato, peeled and cut into ¾-inch cubes

1 medium shallot, thinly sliced

¼ cup extra-virgin olive oil

2 tablespoons freshly squeezed lemon juice

1 tablespoon chopped fresh mint

1 tablespoon chopped fresh parsley

1. Pressure cook the quinoa. Pour the quinoa into the Instant Pot®. Add the stock, or water and salt. Lock the lid into place. Select Manual; adjust the pressure to High and the time to 1 minute. After cooking, naturally release the pressure for 12 minutes, then quick release any remaining pressure. Unlock and remove the lid. Spoon the quinoa into a large bowl and fluff it with a fork. Set aside.

2. Pressure cook the beets and sweet potatoes. Wipe out the pot and pour in the water for steaming. Place the beet and sweet potato cubes in a steamer basket, keeping them separated (or use two small separate steamer baskets). Place the basket(s) in the pot. Lock the lid into place. Select Manual; adjust the pressure to High and the time to 4 minutes. After cooking, naturally release the pressure for 5 minutes, then quick release any remaining pressure. Unlock and remove the lid. Carefully remove the steamer basket(s). Let the beets and sweet potatoes cool.

3. Make the salad. Add the cooled beets and sweet potatoes and the sliced shallot to the quinoa. Drizzle with the olive oil and lemon juice. Toss gently to coat. Taste and add more salt if desired. Top with the mint and parsley and serve.

POLENTA

You can make polenta in the inner pot of an electric pressure cooker, but I find that it's difficult to cook it thoroughly because of scorching. Cooking it in a bowl inside the cooker ensures that it will be deliciously creamy without burning. Even better, there is no constant stirring over the stove top. Enriching the polenta with butter and Parmesan cheese turns it into an exceptional side dish. **SERVES 6**

PREP AND FINISHING
5 minutes

MANUAL
15 minutes
high pressure

RELEASE
Natural for 10 minutes

**TOTAL TIME
35 MINUTES**

60 MIN OR LESS

1 cup polenta or grits (not instant or quick-cooking)

2 cups milk

2 cups Chicken Stock (page 228)

½ teaspoon kosher salt, plus more to taste

1 cup water, for steaming

2 tablespoons unsalted butter

½ cup grated Parmesan or similar cheese

1. Prepare the polenta. In a large bowl (one that holds at least 6 cups), combine the polenta, milk, stock, and salt. Stir.

2. Pressure cook. Pour the water into the Instant Pot®. Place a trivet with handles in the pot and place the bowl on top. If your trivet doesn't have handles, use a foil sling (see page 16) to make removing the bowl easier. Lock the lid into place. Select Manual; adjust the pressure to High and the time to 15 minutes. After cooking, naturally release the pressure for 10 minutes, then quick release any remaining pressure. Unlock and remove the lid.

3. Finish the polenta. Carefully remove the bowl from the Instant Pot®. Add the butter and Parmesan cheese and stir to melt and incorporate. Taste and add more salt if necessary. Serve immediately.

PER SERVING Calories: 201; Fat: 8g; Sodium: 603mg; Carbohydrates: 25g; Fiber: 1g; Protein: 8g

BROWN AND WILD RICE STUFFED PEPPERS

Brown and wild rice are delicious together—the slight crunch of wild rice is a great foil for soft and chewy brown rice. Using the combination for stuffed peppers turns a side dish into a light vegetarian entrée. It's also incredibly versatile and lends itself to many flavors. This recipe is one of my favorites; I find it warm and comforting as the weather turns cooler. **SERVES 4**

PREP AND FINISHING
15 minutes

MANUAL
20 + 8 minutes
high pressure

RELEASE
Natural for
10 + 5 minutes

**TOTAL TIME
1 HOUR**

60 MIN OR LESS

½ cup wild rice

2 cups warm water

4 red or green bell peppers

1 tablespoon extra-virgin olive oil

1 small onion, diced (about ¾ cup)

¼ teaspoon kosher salt, plus more to taste

1 garlic clove, minced

½ cup brown rice

1½ cups Vegetable Stock (page 229)

1 bay leaf

1 fresh thyme sprig or ¼ teaspoon dried thyme

1 cup water, for steaming

½ cup panko bread crumbs

3 tablespoons grated Parmesan or similar cheese

1 tablespoon unsalted butter, melted

1. Soak the wild rice. In a small bowl, combine the wild rice and 2 cups of warm water. Let sit for 15 to 20 minutes, while you prep the remaining ingredients. Drain.

2. Prepare the peppers. Cut about ⅓ inch off the top of each pepper, setting the tops aside. With a paring knife, cut through the ribs on the inside of the peppers and pull out the core. Using the knife and your fingers, remove as much of the ribs as possible, leaving a hollow shell. Set the shells aside. Take the pepper tops and cut away the stems. Trim off any white pithy parts from the inside and dice the flesh. You should have ⅓ to ½ cup of diced bell pepper.

3. Sauté the aromatics. Preheat the Instant Pot® by selecting Sauté and adjust to More for high heat. Heat the olive oil until it shimmers. Add the onion and diced bell pepper and sprinkle with the salt. Cook, stirring frequently, until the onion pieces separate and soften, 2 to 3 minutes. Add the garlic and cook until fragrant, another 1 minute or so.

4. Pressure cook the filling. Add the drained wild rice, the brown rice, the stock, the bay leaf, and the thyme to the pot. Lock the lid into place. Select Manual; adjust the pressure to High and the time to 20 minutes. After cooking, naturally release the pressure for 10 minutes, then quick release any remaining pressure. Unlock and remove the lid. (It's okay if the rice is slightly underdone because it will cook again later.) Adjust the seasoning with more salt if needed, and remove and discard the bay leaf and thyme sprig (if using).

5. Pressure cook the peppers. Spoon the filling into the hollowed-out bell peppers, mounding it up slightly. Wipe out the pot, making sure no rice is stuck to the bottom. Place the steamer trivet in the pot and pour in 1 cup of water. Place the peppers on the trivet. Lock the lid into place. Select Manual; adjust the pressure to High and the time to 8 minutes. After cooking, naturally release the pressure for 5 minutes, then quick release any remaining pressure. Unlock and remove the lid.

6. Finish the dish. Preheat the broiler. Carefully remove the peppers from the pot and place on a baking sheet or in a baking dish. In a small bowl, mix the panko, Parmesan cheese, and melted butter and sprinkle the mixture over the top of the peppers and filling. Broil the peppers until the tops are golden brown and crisp, 2 to 4 minutes. Serve.

PER SERVING Calories: 323; Fat: 10g; Sodium: 626mg; Carbohydrates: 50g; Fiber: 4g; Protein: 10g

SPICY TOFU CURRY WITH RICE (PAGE 113)

CHAPTER 5
MEATLESS MAINS

Even if you're not a full-time vegetarian, you may be looking for recipes for Meatless Mondays, or you might just be interested in reducing the amount of meat you consume. If so, these recipes provide a wide variety of entrées, from American to Mexican to Italian and beyond. And if you're not vegetarian, some of these can be adapted to make great side dishes for meat-based meals. The best part is that vegetables tend to cook more quickly than meat, so most of these recipes will be ready in less than an hour.

RED PEPPER AND TOMATO BISQUE
WITH PARMESAN CROUTONS

It's no wonder that commercial versions of creamy red pepper and tomato soup are so popular—they're like a sophisticated take on the cream of tomato soup so many of us grew up with. My recipe uses no cream; instead, it gets its thick but silky texture from the rice and puréed vegetables, which also give it a uniquely intense flavor. Add the cheesy croutons, and it's a great lunch. Or skip the croutons and serve it with grilled cheese sandwiches for a comforting family dinner. **SERVES 4**

PREP AND FINISHING
20 minutes

MANUAL
12 minutes
high pressure

RELEASE
Natural for 5 minutes

TOTAL TIME
45 MINUTES

60 MIN OR LESS

3 tablespoons extra-virgin olive oil

1 large onion, chopped (about 1½ cups)

3 large garlic cloves, minced

1 teaspoon kosher salt, divided, plus more to taste

⅓ cup dry sherry

2 (14-ounce) cans fire-roasted diced tomatoes, undrained

1 (16-ounce) jar roasted red peppers, drained, blotted dry, and cut into chunks

½ cup strained tomatoes or tomato sauce

½ cup long-grain white rice

2 cups Vegetable Stock (page 229)

8 baguette slices

2 tablespoons unsalted butter, at room temperature

½ cup grated Parmesan or similar cheese

1. Sauté the onions. Preheat the Instant Pot® by selecting Sauté and adjust to More for high heat. Heat the olive oil until it shimmers. Add the onion and garlic and sprinkle with ¼ teaspoon of salt. Cook, stirring frequently, until the onion begins to brown, 3 to 4 minutes.

2. Prepare the remaining ingredients. Add the sherry and cook, scraping up any browned bits from the bottom of the pot, until the liquid has reduced by about half, 3 to 5 minutes. Add the tomatoes with their juice, roasted red peppers, strained tomatoes, rice, vegetable stock, and remaining ¾ teaspoon of salt.

3. Pressure cook. Lock the lid into place. Select Manual; adjust the pressure to High and the time to 12 minutes. After cooking, naturally release the pressure for 5 minutes, then quick release any remaining pressure. Unlock and remove the lid.

4. Make the croutons. Preheat the broiler. Arrange the baguette slices on a baking sheet and butter the top of each slice. Sprinkle with the Parmesan cheese. When the soup has finished cooking and the pressure is releasing, broil the baguette slices until golden brown and bubbling, about 2 minutes.

5. Finish the soup. Purée the soup using an immersion blender. (Alternatively, for a smoother texture, transfer the soup to a countertop blender and purée, working in batches if necessary, then pass through a coarse sieve to remove any tomato or pepper skins. Return to the Instant Pot® to rewarm.) Taste and add more salt if necessary. Ladle the soup into four bowls and top with two croutons each. Serve.

INGREDIENT TIP: If you can't find a 16-ounce jar of roasted red peppers, you can use two 7-ounce jars—that will still be plenty. Or use one whole 12-ounce jar and part of another, reserving the remainder for another use, such as Mussels with Red Pepper–Garlic Sauce (page 129) or Fisherman's Stew (page 124).

PER SERVING Calories: 443; Fat: 21g; Sodium: 1442mg; Carbohydrates: 52g; Fiber: 6g; Protein: 13g

BAKED POTATO SOUP

My partner Dave's family loves broccoli and cheese on baked potatoes, and I've grown to like it as well. In this vegetarian version of baked potato soup, I add a little broccoli for flavor and color and garnish with Cheddar cheese, as well as the more typical baked potato toppings of sour cream and chives. It's definitely comfort food in a bowl. **SERVES 4**

PREP AND FINISHING
15 minutes

MANUAL
0 + 8 minutes
high pressure

RELEASE
Quick + Natural
for 10 minutes

**TOTAL TIME
40 MINUTES**

60 MIN OR LESS

ONE POT

3 russet potatoes (about 2 pounds)

2 cups very small broccoli florets

1 cup water, for steaming

3 tablespoons unsalted butter

½ medium onion, chopped (about ½ cup)

1 tablespoon all-purpose flour

1 teaspoon mustard powder

1 cup milk

2 cups Vegetable Stock (page 229)

½ cup heavy (whipping) cream

1 teaspoon kosher salt, plus more to taste

¼ teaspoon freshly ground black pepper

¼ cup sour cream, for garnish

3 tablespoons minced fresh chives, for garnish

⅔ cup shredded sharp Cheddar cheese, for garnish

1. Prepare the potatoes. Peel the potatoes. Chop one into ½-inch cubes and the other two into 1- to 2-inch chunks. Set aside the larger chunks.

2. Pressure cook the potatoes and broccoli. Put the small (½-inch) potato cubes and the broccoli in a steamer basket. Pour the water into the Instant Pot® and place the steamer basket inside. Lock the lid into place. Select Manual; adjust the pressure to High and the time to 0 minutes. After the pot beeps, quick release the pressure. Unlock and remove the lid. Use tongs or a potholder to remove the steamer basket. Set aside.

3. Prepare the soup. Pour the water out of the pot. Preheat the Instant Pot® by selecting Sauté and adjust to Normal for medium heat. Put the butter in the pot to melt. When it has stopped foaming, add the onion and cook, stirring frequently, until the onion pieces have separated and begun to soften, 2 to 3 minutes. Add the flour and mustard powder and stir to coat the onions. Cook, stirring frequently, until the flour has darkened slightly, about 2 minutes. Add the milk and stir. Bring the liquid to a simmer and cook until the milk is smooth and thickened, about 3 minutes. Add the stock, cream, large potato chunks, and salt. Stir to combine.

4. Pressure cook the soup. Lock the lid into place. Select Manual; adjust the pressure to High and the time to 8 minutes. After cooking, naturally release the pressure for 10 minutes, then quick release any remaining pressure. Unlock and remove the lid.

5. Finish the soup. Use a potato masher to break up the potatoes and thicken the soup. Add the cooked potato and broccoli and let them simmer until warmed through. (Test a piece of potato first; if it's not quite done, add the potatoes to simmer for a couple of minutes before adding the broccoli.) Season with the black pepper and additional salt if necessary. Ladle into bowls, garnish with the sour cream, chives, and cheese, and serve.

COOKING TIP: Steaming some of the potatoes separately (as you'll do in step 2) yields discrete pieces of potato, while the rest melt into the soup to thicken it. If you prefer, you can cook all the potatoes in the soup at once.

PER SERVING Calories: 454; Fat: 25g; Sodium: 830mg; Carbohydrates: 46g; Fiber: 7g; Protein: 13g

VEGETARIAN CHILI VERDE

In my first pressure cooker book, I developed a traditional tomato-and-chili-powder vegetarian chili. It's very good, but I was looking for a change this time around. I thought of chili verde, a green chili, and decided to try that flavor combination with beans and corn instead of pork. This is the result: mild in heat but strong on flavor. If you like a spicier chili, definitely add the chipotle purée. **SERVES 4**

PREP AND FINISHING
15 minutes

MANUAL
15 minutes
high pressure

RELEASE
Natural for 10 minutes

**TOTAL TIME
50 MINUTES,
PLUS OVERNIGHT
TO SOAK**

ONE POT

DAIRY-FREE

1 tablespoon kosher salt, plus ½ teaspoon

1 quart water

8 ounces dried pinto beans

8 ounces dried kidney beans

2 tablespoons extra-virgin olive oil

1 pound tomatillos (5 or 6 large), husked and quartered

1 medium onion, chopped (about 1 cup)

2 garlic cloves, minced

3 cups Vegetable Stock (page 229)

1 (4-ounce) can chopped green chiles, drained

1 teaspoon dried oregano

¼ teaspoon ground cumin

1 jalapeño, seeded and minced

1 cup frozen corn

1 teaspoon chipotle purée (optional; see page 22)

2 to 3 scallions, chopped, for garnish

1 small avocado, peeled, pitted, and diced, for garnish

2 tablespoons chopped fresh cilantro, for garnish

Tortillas or cornbread, for serving

1. Soak the beans. In a large bowl, dissolve 1 tablespoon of salt in the water. Add the pinto and kidney beans and soak at room temperature for 8 to 24 hours. Drain and rinse.

2. Brown the vegetables. Preheat the Instant Pot® by selecting Sauté and adjust to More for high heat. Heat the olive oil until it shimmers. Add the tomatillos in a single layer and cook, undisturbed, until browned, about 2 minutes. Add the onion and garlic and cook, stirring occasionally, until the onion is browned, about 4 minutes.

3. **Prepare the sauce.** Add the vegetable stock and stir, scraping the bottom of the pot to dissolve any browned bits. Add the chiles, oregano, cumin, and remaining ½ teaspoon of salt. Stir to combine.

4. **Pressure cook.** Add the drained beans, jalapeño, and corn to the pot. Lock the lid into place. Select Manual; adjust the pressure to High and the time to 15 minutes. After cooking, naturally release the pressure for 10 minutes, then quick release any remaining pressure. Unlock and remove the lid.

5. **Finish the dish.** Stir in the chipotle purée (if using). If the chili is too soupy, select Sauté and adjust to Normal for medium heat. Simmer until the sauce has thickened to the consistency you want. Taste and adjust the seasoning. Ladle into bowls and garnish with the chopped scallions, avocado, and cilantro. Serve with tortillas or cornbread.

PER SERVING Calories: 595; Fat: 11g; Sodium: 437mg; Carbohydrates: 100g; Fiber: 23g; Protein: 29g

RISOTTO
THREE WAYS

Seeing risotto made in a pressure cooker is what first sold me on the idea of buying one. Under the right circumstances, I don't mind standing and stirring as risotto cooks and thickens. But on busy nights, I don't have the time to devote to the conventional method. After a little prep work, a pressure cooker gives you a huge head start on the process, so you need to stand and stir for only a few minutes to get a perfect risotto. Here is a basic risotto recipe (delicious on its own), plus three variations that build on it to make delicious vegetarian meals, from classic mushrooms and peas to a twist on caprese salad. **SERVES 4**

PREP AND FINISHING
20 minutes

MANUAL
8 minutes
high pressure

RELEASE
Quick

TOTAL TIME
35 MINUTES

60 MIN OR LESS

ONE POT

CORE INGREDIENTS

3 tablespoons unsalted butter, divided

½ small onion, chopped (about ½ cup)

1 cup Arborio rice

⅓ cup dry white wine

2¾ to 3 cups Vegetable Stock (page 229), divided

½ teaspoon kosher salt

⅓ cup grated Parmesan or similar cheese

FOR MUSHROOM-PEA RISOTTO

6 ounces white button or cremini mushrooms, sliced

1 cup frozen peas, thawed

FOR BUTTERNUT SQUASH RISOTTO

1 cup (½-inch) butternut squash cubes

½ teaspoon crumbled dried sage

FOR CAPRESE RISOTTO

1 medium tomato, seeded and diced

2 tablespoons chiffonade basil (see Tip)

¼ cup (¼-inch) fresh mozzarella cubes

1. Sauté the vegetables and rice. Preheat the Instant Pot® by selecting Sauté and adjust to Normal for medium heat. Put 2 tablespoons of butter in the pot to melt. When it has stopped foaming, add the onion.

For the Mushroom-Pea Risotto: Add the mushrooms and cook, stirring frequently, until the onion pieces separate and soften, 2 to 3 minutes.

For Butternut Squash Risotto: Add the butternut squash and sage and cook, stirring frequently, until the onion pieces separate and soften, 2 to 3 minutes.

For Caprese Risotto: Cook, stirring frequently, until the onion pieces separate and soften, 2 to 3 minutes.

For all variations: Add the rice and stir to coat in the butter, cooking it for about 1 minute. Add the wine and cook, stirring occasionally, until it's almost evaporated, 2 to 3 minutes.

2. **Pressure cook.** Add 2½ cups of stock and the salt to the pot and stir to combine. Lock the lid into place. Select Manual; adjust the pressure to High and the time to 8 minutes. After cooking, quick release the pressure. Unlock and remove the lid.

3. **Finish the risotto.** Test the risotto; the rice should be soft with a slightly firm center, and the sauce should be creamy. If the rice is not quite done, add another ¼ to ½ cup of stock and simmer until it is done, 2 to 3 minutes. If the rice is done but too dry, add enough stock to loosen it up. Stir in the remaining 1 tablespoon of butter and the Parmesan cheese. Taste and add more salt if necessary.

For Mushroom-Pea Risotto: Add the peas and stir until they are heated through.

For Caprese Risotto: Gently stir in the tomato, basil, and mozzarella. Serve.

PER SERVING Calories: 312; Fat: 11g; Sodium: 531mg; Carbohydrates: 41g; Fiber: 2g; Protein: 7g

PER SERVING (MUSHROOM-PEA RISOTTO VARIATION) Calories: 353; Fat: 12g; Sodium: 562mg; Carbohydrates: 48g; Fiber: 5g; Protein: 11g

PER SERVING (BUTTERNUT SQUASH RISOTTO VARIATION) Calories: 328; Fat: 11g; Sodium: 532mg; Carbohydrates: 46g; Fiber: 3g; Protein: 8g

PER SERVING (CAPRESE RISOTTO VARIATION) Calories: 335; Fat: 13g; Sodium: 574mg; Carbohydrates: 42g; Fiber: 3g; Protein: 10g

PREP TIP: For the basil chiffonade, stack several basil leaves in a pile and roll them up lengthwise. Use a sharp knife to cut thin strips crosswise to form ribbons (which is what "chiffonade" means).

VEGETARIAN LASAGNA

Lasagna never appealed to me until I had a version made with fresh pasta. It also contained *balsamella* (also known as béchamel, or white sauce) instead of the more typical ricotta mixture, and much less mozzarella than any I'd tasted before. That version was the inspiration for this recipe. Since fresh pasta can be difficult to find, I call for egg roll wrappers, but if you can find sheets of fresh pasta, feel free to use them. **SERVES 4**

PREP AND FINISHING
30 minutes

MANUAL
20 minutes
high pressure

RELEASE
Natural for 10 minutes

TOTAL TIME
1 HOUR 10 MINUTES

FOR THE BALSAMELLA

4 tablespoons unsalted butter

¼ cup all-purpose flour

1½ cups whole milk

¼ teaspoon kosher salt

¼ teaspoon freshly ground white or black pepper

FOR THE LASAGNA

2 tablespoons extra-virgin olive oil

8 ounces white button or cremini mushrooms, sliced

1 cup diced eggplant (about ½ medium eggplant)

½ teaspoon kosher salt

Unsalted butter, at room temperature

2 cups Arrabbiata Sauce (page 237)

1 (8-ounce) package egg roll wrappers

3 ounces Parmesan or similar cheese, coarsely grated

½ cup shredded whole-milk mozzarella or provolone cheese

1 cup water, for steaming

1. Make the balsamella. Heat the butter in a medium saucepan over medium heat until it melts. Once it stops foaming, whisk in the flour all at once, stirring to make it smooth. Add the milk, a little at a time, continuing to whisk. Once all the milk is added, bring the sauce to a low simmer. Stir in the salt and pepper. Simmer for 10 minutes, stirring often, then remove from the heat. Set aside.

2. Brown the vegetables. Preheat the Instant Pot® by selecting Sauté and adjust to More for high heat. Heat the oil until it shimmers. Add the mushrooms and eggplant and sprinkle with the salt. Cook, stirring frequently, until the vegetables release their liquid and begin to brown, about 5 minutes. Transfer the vegetables to a bowl and rinse out the pot. ➤

3. **Prepare the lasagna.** Lightly coat the bottom of a 1-quart baking dish with butter and spread a spoonful of arrabbiata sauce over the bottom of the dish. Add a layer of egg roll wrappers, overlapping them as little as possible and trimming the edges so they fit. Spoon some arrabbiata sauce over the wrappers. Scatter some mushrooms and eggplant over the sauce, then dot them with dollops of balsamella (a small ice cream scoop is useful here) and dust with the Parmesan cheese. Repeat these layers (wrappers, sauce, vegetables, balsamella) as many more times as you have room for, ending with a layer of egg roll wrappers. Press each layer of wrappers onto the fillings underneath it, which will even out the balsamella (you likely won't use all the wrappers in the package). Be sure to leave enough arrabbiata sauce to spread on top of the final wrapper layer. Top with the mozzarella cheese. Place a sheet of aluminum foil over the top and crimp it lightly.

4. **Pressure cook.** Pour the water into the Instant Pot®. Place a trivet with handles in the pot and place the baking dish on top. If your trivet doesn't have handles, use a foil sling (see page 16) to make removing the dish easier. Lock the lid into place. Select Manual; adjust the pressure to High and the time to 20 minutes. After cooking, naturally release the pressure for 10 minutes, then quick release any remaining pressure. Unlock and remove the lid.

5. **Finish the lasagna.** If you like, place the lasagna under a preheated broiler until the cheese is browned on the top, 2 to 3 minutes. Regardless, let the lasagna rest for 10 to 15 minutes before serving, to allow it to set.

PER SERVING Calories: 629; Fat: 35g; Sodium: 1507mg; Carbohydrates: 57g; Fiber: 6g; Protein: 25g

SPICY TOFU CURRY
WITH RICE

I wouldn't have thought of pressure cooking tofu had I not read a *Washington Post* article about Jill Nussinow's book *Vegan Under Pressure*. It turns out that tofu cooks very quickly, so this spicy dish can be finished in the time it takes to make rice to go along with it. Meatless Mondays don't get easier or more delicious than this! **SERVES 4**

PREP AND FINISHING
15 minutes

MANUAL
4 minutes
high pressure

RELEASE
Quick

TOTAL TIME
25 MINUTES

30 MIN OR LESS

ONE POT

DAIRY-FREE

1 tablespoon extra-virgin olive oil

1 medium onion, chopped

3 garlic cloves, finely minced

1 small red bell pepper, seeded and chopped

½ teaspoon kosher salt, divided

¾ cup Vegetable Stock (page 229)

2 tablespoons tomato paste

1 (14-ounce) can diced tomatoes, drained

1 tablespoon freshly squeezed lime juice

1 teaspoon Thai red curry paste

1 teaspoon curry powder

1 teaspoon sugar

1 pound firm or extra-firm tofu, drained and cut into ½-inch cubes

2 cups cooked white rice, for serving

2 scallions, sliced, for garnish

1. **Sauté the vegetables.** Preheat the Instant Pot® by selecting Sauté and adjust to More for high heat. Heat the oil until it shimmers. Add the onion, garlic, and red bell pepper and sprinkle with ¼ teaspoon of salt. Cook, stirring frequently, until the onion pieces separate and begin to soften, 2 to 3 minutes.

2. **Pressure cook.** Stir in the vegetable stock, tomato paste, and tomatoes and stir to break up the tomato paste. Add the lime juice, curry paste, curry powder, and sugar and stir to combine. Add the tofu. Lock the lid into place. Select Manual; adjust the pressure to High and the time to 4 minutes. After cooking, quick release the pressure. Unlock and remove the lid.

3. **Finish the dish.** Stir the curry, then let it sit for 2 to 3 minutes. Serve over rice and garnish with the scallions.

PER SERVING Calories: 343; Fat: 10g; Sodium: 341mg; Carbohydrates: 52g; Fiber: 5g; Protein: 15g

PENNE CAPONATA

Caponata is a traditional Italian sweet and sour eggplant dish. It is usually served at room temperature as a topping for crostini or as a relish-like side dish. But I've found that it's also great served warm with pasta for an unusual but delicious meatless entrée. **SERVES 4**

PREP AND FINISHING
10 minutes

MANUAL
5 minutes
high pressure

RELEASE
Quick

TOTAL TIME
20 MINUTES

30 MIN OR LESS

ONE POT

2 tablespoons extra-virgin olive oil

1 medium onion, chopped

3 large garlic cloves, minced

1 teaspoon kosher salt, divided, plus more to taste

1 medium eggplant, chopped

1 large celery stalk, sliced

1 large red bell pepper, seeded and chopped

1 (14-ounce) can diced tomatoes, undrained

3 tablespoons red wine vinegar, divided

3 tablespoons drained capers, divided

2 tablespoons sliced green olives, divided

2 tablespoons sugar

6 ounces penne

1 cup water

1 tablespoon minced fresh basil

¼ cup grated Parmesan or similar cheese

1. Start the caponata. Preheat the Instant Pot® by selecting Sauté and adjust to More for high heat. Heat the oil until it shimmers. Add the onion and garlic and sprinkle with ¼ teaspoon of salt. Cook, stirring frequently, until the onion pieces separate and begin to soften, 2 to 3 minutes. Add the eggplant, celery, and red bell pepper and cook, stirring frequently, for 1 minute. Add the tomatoes with their juice, 2 tablespoons of vinegar, 1 tablespoon of capers, 1 tablespoon of green olives, and the sugar. Stir to combine.

2. **Pressure cook the pasta.** Add the pasta, water, and remaining ¾ teaspoon of salt. Stir to combine. Lock the lid into place. Select Manual; adjust the pressure to High and the time to 5 minutes. After cooking, quick release the pressure. Unlock and remove the lid. Test the pasta; it should be tender with just a slightly firm center. If it's not done enough, simmer for 1 to 2 minutes until done to your liking.

3. **Finish the dish.** Add the remaining 1 tablespoon of vinegar, 2 tablespoons of capers, and 1 tablespoon of olives, and taste, adding more salt if necessary. The dish should have a good balance of sweet and sour flavors. Stir in the basil and Parmesan cheese and serve.

PER SERVING Calories: 309; Fat: 11g; Sodium: 930mg; Carbohydrates: 47g; Fiber: 7g; Protein: 10g

SMOKY BLACK BEAN TACOS

If you want a change from your usual taco night, try this black bean filling instead of ground beef or chicken. It's a little spicy, a little smoky, and very tasty. Plus, once the beans are soaked, it cooks very quickly—perfect for weeknight tacos! Leftovers freeze well, too; just defrost and warm them up to use for another meal. **SERVES 4**

PREP AND FINISHING
20 minutes

MANUAL
15 minutes
high pressure

RELEASE
Natural for 10 minutes

**TOTAL TIME
50 MINUTES,
PLUS OVERNIGHT
TO SOAK**

ONE POT

1 tablespoon plus 1 teaspoon kosher salt, divided

1 quart water

12 ounces dried black beans

1 tablespoon extra-virgin olive oil

1 small onion, chopped (about ¾ cup)

1 medium jalapeño, seeded and diced

½ small red bell pepper, chopped (about ¼ cup)

½ small green bell pepper, chopped (about ¼ cup)

2 medium garlic cloves, minced

2½ cups Vegetable Stock (page 229)

2 tablespoons Ancho Chile Sauce (page 239)

1 teaspoon chipotle purée (see page 22)

1 teaspoon ground cumin

½ teaspoon dried oregano

8 to 12 corn or flour tortillas, warmed

1 cup crumbled queso fresco or shredded Monterey Jack cheese

FOR THE PICO DE GALLO

1 large tomato, seeded and diced

½ very small onion, chopped (about ⅓ cup)

1 large jalapeño, seeded and chopped (about 3 tablespoons)

2 tablespoons chopped fresh cilantro

⅛ teaspoon ground cumin

½ teaspoon kosher salt, or more to taste

1 to 2 teaspoons freshly squeezed lime juice, divided

1. **Soak the beans.** In a large bowl, dissolve 1 tablespoon of kosher salt in the water. Add the beans and soak at room temperature for 8 to 24 hours. Drain and rinse.

2. **Brown the vegetables.** Preheat the Instant Pot® by selecting Sauté and adjust to More for high heat. Heat the olive oil until it shimmers. Add the onion, jalapeño, red and green bell peppers, and garlic. Cook, stirring occasionally, until the onion is softened, 2 to 3 minutes. Add the vegetable stock and stir, scraping the bottom of the pot to dissolve any browned bits. Stir in the chile sauce, chipotle purée, cumin, oregano, and remaining 1 teaspoon of salt.

3. **Pressure cook.** Add the drained beans to the pot. Lock the lid into place. Select Manual; adjust the pressure to High and the time to 15 minutes. After cooking, naturally release the pressure for 10 minutes, then quick release any remaining pressure. Unlock and remove the lid.

4. **Make the pico de gallo.** While the beans are cooking, in a small bowl, gently toss together the diced tomato, onion, jalapeño, cilantro, cumin, salt, and 1 teaspoon of lime juice. Taste and adjust the seasoning, adding the remaining 1 teaspoon of lime juice if necessary.

5. **Finish the dish.** If the beans are too soupy, select Sauté and adjust to Normal for medium heat. Simmer until the sauce has thickened to the consistency you want. Taste and add more salt if necessary. To serve, spoon some beans into a warmed tortilla and top with the cheese and pico de gallo.

PER SERVING Calories: 624; Fat: 16g; Sodium: 1140mg; Carbohydrates: 94g; Fiber: 20g; Protein: 31g

CHEESY SHELLS
WITH ARTICHOKES AND SPINACH

Think of this dish as a delicious cross between pasta Alfredo and the always-popular spinach-artichoke dip. It's quite rich, but the slight bitterness of the artichokes and the tang of lemon help balance the creaminess. You can use frozen spinach instead of fresh if you have it on hand; just be sure to thaw it and squeeze it dry before adding. **SERVES 4**

PREP AND FINISHING
20 minutes

MANUAL
5 minutes
low pressure

RELEASE
Quick

TOTAL TIME
35 MINUTES

60 MIN OR LESS

ONE POT

1½ cups water

1 (12-ounce) can evaporated milk, divided

8 ounces shell pasta

12 ounces frozen artichoke hearts, thawed and cut into bite-size pieces

3 large garlic cloves, minced

2 tablespoons unsalted butter

1 teaspoon kosher salt

1 large egg

1 teaspoon grated lemon zest

2 teaspoons freshly squeezed lemon juice

¼ teaspoon freshly ground black pepper

9 to 10 ounces baby spinach

4 ounces Parmesan or similar cheese, grated (about 1⅓ cups)

¼ cup heavy (whipping) cream, plus more to taste

1. Pressure cook. Pour the water and ¾ cup of evaporated milk into the Instant Pot®. Add the pasta, artichoke hearts, garlic, butter, and salt and stir to combine, submerging the pasta in the liquid. Lock the lid into place. Select Manual; adjust the pressure to Low and the time to 5 minutes. After cooking, quick release the pressure. Unlock and remove the lid.

2. **Finish the dish.** In a small bowl, whisk together the remaining ¾ cup of evaporated milk and the egg (you can do this while the noodles cook). Select Sauté and adjust to Less for low heat. Pour the milk mixture into the noodles and cook, stirring occasionally, until the sauce has thickened. Add the lemon zest, lemon juice, and black pepper and stir to combine. Add the spinach and Parmesan cheese. Cook, stirring occasionally, until the spinach wilts and the cheese melts. Stir in the cream, adding more if the sauce is too thick. Serve immediately.

INGREDIENT TIP: If you happen to have leftover cooked mushrooms in the refrigerator, they would make an excellent addition to this dish.

PER SERVING Calories: 524; Fat: 24g; Sodium: 1148mg; Carbohydrates: 53g; Fiber: 6g; Protein: 28g

PEEL-AND-EAT SHRIMP WITH TWO SAUCES (PAGE 122)

CHAPTER 6

FISH & SHELLFISH

With seafood, pressure cooking is tricky. Much seafood overcooks so quickly that even the shortest time on high pressure can turn fish to mush or shrimp to rubber. But where there's a will, there's a way. Beginning with frozen fish or shellfish can provide a time cushion and result in perfectly cooked seafood. And with most fish, low pressure and quick release are your best friends. (If your Instant Pot® doesn't have a low pressure setting, cut a minute off the cooking time.) More so than with beef, pork, or even chicken, a couple of extra minutes in the pressure cooker can spell disaster for fish and shellfish. Thus, it's crucial to obey the cooking time, water amounts for steaming, and pressure release details for these recipes.

PEEL-AND-EAT SHRIMP
WITH TWO SAUCES

I know what you're thinking—shrimp in a pressure cooker? Won't they be over-cooked? That's exactly what I thought at first, until I started experimenting with shrimp frozen in the shell. Turns out that if they go in frozen, protected by their shells, shrimp can turn out perfectly. Make a couple of classic sauces while the shrimp cook and cool, and you have a great appetizer for any occasion. **SERVES 4**

PREP AND FINISHING
15 minutes

STEAM
1 minute
low pressure

RELEASE
Quick

TOTAL TIME
20 MINUTES

30 MIN OR LESS

ONE POT

GRAIN-FREE

CORE INGREDIENTS

1 cup water, for steaming

2 pounds frozen jumbo (16/25) shrimp, shell on

FOR THE COCKTAIL SAUCE

½ cup ketchup

1 tablespoon prepared horseradish

1 tablespoon freshly squeezed lemon juice

½ teaspoon Worcestershire sauce

Dash hot pepper sauce, such as Tabasco

⅛ teaspoon celery salt

FOR THE REMOULADE

¼ cup plain Yogurt (page 230)

¼ cup mayonnaise

2 tablespoons ketchup

2 tablespoons Creole mustard or other grainy mustard

2 teaspoons prepared horseradish

½ teaspoon Worcestershire sauce

2 scallions, roughly chopped

2 tablespoons fresh parsley leaves

1. Make an ice bath. Fill a large bowl about halfway with cold water. Add several handfuls of ice cubes. Set aside.

2. Pressure cook the shrimp. Pour the water into the Instant Pot®. Arrange the frozen shrimp in a single layer (as much as possible) in a steamer basket and place it inside. Lock the lid into place. Select Steam; adjust the pressure to Low and the time to 1 minute. After cooking, quick release the pressure.

3. Cool the shrimp. Immediately unlock and remove the lid and take the steamer basket out. Transfer the shrimp to the ice bath.

4. Make the sauce. Follow the instructions below for the sauces.

To make the cocktail sauce: In a small bowl, mix the ketchup, horseradish, lemon juice, Worcestershire sauce, hot sauce, and celery salt. Whisk until smooth and adjust the seasoning, if necessary.

To make the remoulade: Place the yogurt, mayonnaise, ketchup, mustard, horseradish, Worcestershire sauce, scallions, and parsley in a small food processor. Process until mostly smooth, scraping down the sides of the bowl as necessary. (If you don't have a food processor, whisk together the yogurt, mayonnaise, ketchup, mustard, horseradish, and Worcestershire sauce. Finely mince the scallions and parsley and stir into the sauce.)

5. Serve. Arrange the shrimp on a large platter with the dipping sauces in ramekins. Provide a bowl for the shells—and lots of napkins.

INGREDIENT TIP: If your shrimp are smaller, follow the same procedure but cook for 0 minutes at low pressure. The smallest-size shrimp I recommend for this recipe is 26/30.

PER SERVING Calories: 409; Fat: 11g; Sodium: 1127mg; Carbohydrates: 21g; Fiber: 1g; Protein: 55g

FISHERMAN'S STEW
(BOUILLABAISSE)

Bouillabaisse is one of those dishes that started out as a rustic, thrown-together soup made with whatever was left over from the day's catch. A classic from the French Mediterranean coast, it's turned into an involved, all-day affair with half a dozen types of seafood. This version, although it calls for a rather long list of ingredients, is streamlined quite a bit. It comes together quickly, and with just shrimp and one type of fish, it strikes the perfect balance between rustic and elegant. **SERVES 4**

PREP AND FINISHING
15 minutes

MANUAL
10 minutes high +
1 minute low pressure

RELEASE
Natural for
5 minutes + Quick

**TOTAL TIME
35 MINUTES**

60 MIN OR LESS

ONE POT

DAIRY-FREE

2 tablespoons extra-virgin olive oil

½ small onion, chopped (about ½ cup)

½ small fennel bulb, trimmed and chopped (about ½ cup)

1 small garlic clove, minced

1 (14-ounce) can diced tomatoes, undrained

3 cups fish stock, clam juice, or water

½ cup dry white wine

Zest and juice of 1 orange (zest removed in large strips)

1 bay leaf

½ teaspoon kosher salt (1 teaspoon if using water)

¼ teaspoon freshly ground black pepper

3 or 4 saffron threads (optional)

12 ounces firm white fish fillets, such as cod, halibut, or snapper

12 ounces peeled medium-large (36/40) frozen shrimp

2 tablespoons chopped fresh parsley

Toasted baguette slices, for serving

FOR THE ROUILLE

3 tablespoons mayonnaise

1 tablespoon extra-virgin olive oil

¼ cup finely chopped roasted red pepper

½ teaspoon minced garlic

1. **Prepare the base.** Preheat the Instant Pot® by selecting Sauté and adjust to Normal for medium heat. Heat the olive oil until it shimmers. Add the onion, fennel, and garlic and cook, stirring frequently, until the garlic is fragrant, about 1 minute. Add the tomatoes with their juice, fish stock, wine, orange zest and juice, bay leaf, salt, pepper, and saffron (if using). Stir to combine.

2. **Pressure cook the base.** Lock the lid into place. Select Manual; adjust the pressure to High and the time to 10 minutes. After cooking, naturally release the pressure for 5 minutes, then quick release any remaining pressure. Unlock and remove the lid.

3. **Make the rouille:** While the soup base is cooking, combine the mayonnaise, oil, red pepper, and garlic in a deep narrow container and blend with an immersion blender. (If you don't have an immersion blender, simply whisk together the ingredients in a small bowl—the sauce won't be as smooth, but it will taste fine.)

4. **Pressure cook the fish.** Add the fish fillets and shrimp to the soup. Lock the lid into place. Select Manual; adjust the pressure to Low and the time to 1 minute. After cooking, quick release the pressure. Unlock and remove the lid.

5. **Finish the dish.** Remove and discard the bay leaf and strips of orange zest. Stir in the parsley. Ladle into bowls and top each with a spoonful of rouille. Serve with toasted baguette slices.

PER SERVING Calories: 409; Fat: 17g; Sodium: 1018mg; Carbohydrates: 18g; Fiber: 3g; Protein: 41g

TILAPIA
THREE WAYS

Tilapia is among America's most popular fishes. It cooks quickly, and its mild flavor makes it a great base for all kinds of cuisines. Cooking frozen tilapia in the pressure cooker results in fish that's perfectly cooked—and you can make any number of sauces at the same time. These are some of my favorites. **SERVES 4**

PREP AND FINISHING
15 minutes

MANUAL
2 minutes
low pressure

RELEASE
Quick

**TOTAL TIME
25 MINUTES**

30 MIN OR LESS

ONE POT

GRAIN-FREE

CORE INGREDIENTS
4 (4- to 5-ounce) frozen tilapia fillets

½ teaspoon kosher salt

Cooking spray

FOR PARSLEY-CAPER SAUCE
2 tablespoons extra-virgin olive oil

1 large garlic clove, minced

1 scallion, thinly sliced

½ cup Vegetable Stock (page 229)

1 tablespoon dry white wine

2 tablespoons drained capers

¼ cup chopped fresh parsley

FOR TOMATO-OLIVE SAUCE
2 tablespoons extra-virgin olive oil

1 large garlic clove, minced

1 large shallot, sliced, or ¼ cup sliced onion

1 tablespoon dry white wine

1 (14-ounce) can diced tomatoes, undrained

¼ cup sliced green olives

1 tablespoon chopped fresh parsley

FOR MUSTARD-CHIVE SAUCE
2 tablespoons unsalted butter

1 large garlic clove, minced

1 large shallot, sliced, or ¼ cup sliced onion

¼ cup heavy (whipping) cream

¼ cup Vegetable Stock (page 229)

1 tablespoon dry white wine

2 tablespoons Dijon-style mustard

2 tablespoons minced fresh chives

PER SERVING Calories: 118; Fat: 1g; Sodium: 341mg; Carbohydrates: 0g; Fiber: 0g; Protein: 26g

PER SERVING (PARSLEY-CAPER SAUCE VARIATION) Calories: 187; Fat: 9g; Sodium: 567mg; Carbohydrates: 1g; Fiber: 0g; Protein: 27g

PER SERVING (TOMATO-OLIVE SAUCE VARIATION) Calories: 220; Fat: 10g; Sodium: 549mg; Carbohydrates: 6g; Fiber: 2g; Protein: 28g

PER SERVING (MUSTARD-CHIVE SAUCE VARIATION) Calories: 228; Fat: 12g; Sodium: 433mg; Carbohydrates: 3g; Fiber: 1g; Protein: 28g

1. **Prepare the fish.** Sprinkle both sides of the fillets with the salt. Spray a silicone steamer trivet with cooking spray and arrange the frozen fillets in a single layer (as much as possible) on it.

2. **Prepare the sauce.**

For Parsley-Caper Sauce: Combine the olive oil, garlic, scallion, stock, and wine in the Instant Pot®.

For Tomato-Olive Sauce: Combine the olive oil, garlic, shallot, wine, and tomatoes with their juice in the pot.

For Mustard-Chive Sauce: Combine the butter, garlic, shallot, cream, stock, and wine in the pot.

3. **Pressure cook the fish.** Place the trivet with the fish in the pot. Lock the lid into place. Select Manual; adjust the pressure to Low and the time to 2 minutes. After cooking, quick release the pressure. Unlock and remove the lid.

4. **Finish the dish.** Carefully remove the trivet and loosely tent the fish with aluminum foil to keep it warm. Select Sauté and adjust to Normal for medium heat.

For Parsley-Caper Sauce: Simmer the sauce until most of the liquid has evaporated. Stir in the capers and parsley.

For Tomato-Olive Sauce: Simmer the sauce until about half of the liquid has evaporated. Stir in the olives and parsley.

For Mustard-Chive Sauce: Stir in the mustard and chives.

5. **Serve the fish.** Arrange the fillets on a serving platter and spoon the sauce over them. Serve.

MUSSELS
WITH RED PEPPER–GARLIC SAUCE

There's something comforting about digging into a big bowl of steamed mussels with a savory broth. In this recipe, the roasted red pepper gives a hint of sweetness to the broth, which complements the mussels perfectly. It's also fabulous for sopping up with plenty of crusty bread. It's definitely one of those dishes that will impress anyone you serve it to—despite how easy it is to make! **SERVES 4**

PREP AND FINISHING
15 minutes

MANUAL
1 minute
high pressure

RELEASE
Quick

TOTAL TIME
20 MINUTES

30 MIN OR LESS

ONE POT

GRAIN-FREE

3 pounds mussels

1 tablespoon extra-virgin olive oil

4 garlic cloves, minced

1 large roasted red bell pepper, minced or puréed

¾ cup fish stock, clam juice, or water

½ cup dry white wine

⅛ teaspoon red pepper flakes

2 tablespoons heavy (whipping) cream

3 tablespoons coarsely chopped fresh parsley

1. Clean the mussels. Scrub the mussels and debeard if necessary (some fish counters sell debearded mussels).

2. Make the steaming liquid. Preheat the Instant Pot® by selecting Sauté and adjust to Normal for medium heat. Heat the olive oil until it shimmers. Add the garlic and cook, stirring frequently, until it is fragrant, about 1 minute. Add the roasted red pepper, fish stock, wine, and red pepper flakes. Stir to combine.

3. Pressure cook. Add the mussels to the pot. Lock the lid into place. Select Manual; adjust the pressure to High and the time to 1 minute. After cooking, quick release the pressure. Unlock and remove the lid. Check the mussels; if they are not opened, replace the lid but don't lock it into place. Let the mussels steam for another 1 minute, until they've opened. (Discard any that do not open.)

4. Finish the dish. Stir in the cream and parsley and serve with the cooking liquid.

PER SERVING Calories: 388; Fat: 14g; Sodium: 980mg; Carbohydrates: 17g; Fiber: 1g; Protein: 41g

STEAMED COD
WITH GINGER-GARLIC BROTH AND SNOW PEAS

Steamed whole fish topped with a flavorful mixture of vegetables, herbs, and spices is a classic Chinese dish, but a whole fish isn't always practical for the home cook. Fillets to the rescue! This recipe combines fish fillets and crunchy snow peas with a deliciously aromatic broth for an easy adaptation of the classic. **SERVES 4**

PREP AND FINISHING
10 minutes

MANUAL
2 minutes
low pressure

RELEASE
Quick

TOTAL TIME
20 MINUTES

30 MIN OR LESS

ONE POT

DAIRY-FREE

4 (6- to 8-ounce) cod fillets

¼ teaspoon kosher salt

¼ teaspoon freshly ground black pepper

1 cup fish stock or Vegetable Stock (page 229)

2 tablespoons unseasoned rice vinegar

2 tablespoons soy sauce

2 tablespoons dry sherry or rice wine

1 tablespoon minced peeled ginger

2 or 3 large garlic cloves, minced (about 1 tablespoon)

8 ounces snow peas, trimmed

2 scallions, thinly sliced

1 tablespoon toasted sesame oil

1. Prepare the fish and broth. Season the cod on both sides with the salt and pepper. Combine the stock, vinegar, soy sauce, sherry, ginger, and garlic in the Instant Pot®. Place a steamer trivet or basket in the pot and place the cod on it. Scatter the snow peas over the fillets.

2. Pressure cook. Lock the lid into place. Select Manual; adjust the pressure to Low and the time to 2 minutes. After cooking, quick release the pressure. Unlock and remove the lid. Carefully remove the steamer trivet from the pot.

3. Finish the dish. With a large slotted spatula, divide the fish and snow peas among four shallow bowls. Spoon the broth over the fish. Top with the scallions, drizzle with the sesame oil, and serve.

INGREDIENT TIP: If you're using frozen cod fillets, increase the cooking time to 3 minutes.

PER SERVING Calories: 318; Fat: 6g; Sodium: 871mg; Carbohydrates: 7g; Fiber: 2g; Protein: 56g

POACHED SALMON
WITH MUSTARD CREAM SAUCE

As I discovered when I was researching my first pressure cooker cookbook, pressure poaching salmon is an easy and delicious way to prepare it. I borrowed the idea of lightly whipping cream for the sauce from a *New York Times* recipe by David Tanis—it lightens the texture of the sauce and pairs beautifully with the rich fish. **SERVES 4**

PREP AND FINISHING
15 minutes

MANUAL
5 minutes
low pressure

RELEASE
Quick

**TOTAL TIME
25 MINUTES**

30 MIN OR LESS

ONE POT

GRAIN-FREE

1 (20- to 24-ounce) center-cut salmon fillet

1 teaspoon kosher salt, divided

½ teaspoon freshly ground black pepper, divided

2 cups water or fish stock

½ cup dry white wine

Zest and juice of 1 small lemon

1 bay leaf

⅓ cup heavy (whipping) cream

1 tablespoon Dijon-style mustard

3 tablespoons minced fresh dill, divided

1. Prepare the fish and poaching liquid. Season the salmon with ½ teaspoon of salt and ¼ teaspoon of black pepper. Combine the water, wine, lemon zest and juice, and bay leaf in the Instant Pot®. Place a steamer trivet or basket in the pot and place the salmon on top of it. The fish should be partially submerged in the liquid.

2. Pressure cook. Lock the lid into place. Select Manual; adjust the pressure to Low and the time to 5 minutes. After cooking, quick release the pressure. Unlock and remove the lid.

3. Make the sauce. While the fish is cooking, pour the cream into a small bowl and beat with a hand mixer or vigorously whisk by hand just until the cream has thickened. Stir in the mustard, the remaining ½ teaspoon of salt and ¼ teaspoon of pepper, and 2 tablespoons of dill.

4. Finish the dish. Carefully remove the steamer trivet from the pot. With a large slotted spatula, transfer the fish to a platter. Spoon the sauce over the fish, garnish it with the remaining 1 tablespoon of dill, and serve.

PER SERVING Calories: 322; Fat: 16g; Sodium: 848mg; Carbohydrates: 3g; Fiber: 1g; Protein: 37g

FISH & SHELLFISH

CREAMY CORN CHOWDER
WITH SMOKED TROUT

Years ago, my then boyfriend got the book *Beer Cuisine* by Jay Harlow for his birthday. It had quite a few great recipes, which I (not he) cooked, including one for pasta with smoked trout and corn. When we split up, he kept the book (of course). By then, though, I'd adapted the combination of smoky fish and sweet corn in a creamy sauce to all kinds of other dishes, including this unusual chowder. **SERVES 4**

PREP AND FINISHING
15 minutes

MANUAL
5 minutes
high pressure

RELEASE
Natural for 5 minutes

TOTAL TIME
35 MINUTES

60 MIN OR LESS

ONE POT

1 tablespoon unsalted butter

2 large scallions, chopped (about ⅓ cup)

½ teaspoon kosher salt, plus more to taste

1 tablespoon all-purpose flour

¼ cup dry white wine

3 cups whole milk

2 small or 1 medium Yukon gold potato, peeled and cut into ½-inch cubes (about 2 cups)

1½ cups frozen corn

2 tablespoons sour cream

2 teaspoons prepared horseradish

1 teaspoon grated lemon zest

4 ounces hot-smoked trout, chopped or flaked into small chunks

2 tablespoons chopped fresh chives

Freshly ground black pepper

1. Make the soup base. Preheat the Instant Pot® by selecting Sauté and adjust to Normal for medium heat. Put the butter in the pot to melt. When it has stopped foaming, add the scallions and sprinkle them with the salt. Cook, stirring frequently, until softened, about 1 minute. Stir in the flour and cook until it turns a very light tan color, 2 to 3 minutes. Add the wine, whisking to combine with the flour mixture, and cook until the mixture has thickened, about 2 minutes. Add the milk and whisk until the mixture is smooth.

2. **Pressure cook the soup.** Add the potatoes and corn. Lock the lid into place. Select Manual; adjust the pressure to High and the time to 5 minutes. After cooking, naturally release the pressure for 5 minutes, then quick release any remaining pressure. Unlock and remove the lid.

3. **Finish the soup.** Add the sour cream, horseradish, and lemon zest. Stir and taste, adding more salt and black pepper if necessary. Stir in the trout and ladle the soup into bowls. Top with the chives and serve.

INGREDIENT TIP: If you can't find smoked trout, substitute smoked salmon. Just be sure to buy the hot-smoked variety, not lox.

PER SERVING Calories: 308; Fat: 13g; Sodium: 428mg; Carbohydrates: 30g; Fiber: 3g; Protein: 17g

TUNA NOODLE CASSEROLE

Tuna noodle casserole, despite its name and background, is actually better cooked on the stove or in a pressure cooker than in the oven in a casserole dish, which always seems to produce overcooked noodles and dried-out tuna. This version is decidedly rich and creamy, with a tangy background from the sour cream. Since the tuna and peas are added at the end, the tuna stays fresh tasting and the peas crisp-tender rather than mushy. **SERVES 4**

PREP AND FINISHING
15 minutes

MANUAL
5 minutes
low pressure

RELEASE
Quick

TOTAL TIME
25 MINUTES

30 MIN OR LESS

ONE POT

1 tablespoon vegetable oil

1 medium onion, chopped (about 1 cup)

1 large celery stalk, chopped (about ½ cup)

6 ounces wide egg noodles

1 (12-ounce) can evaporated milk, divided

1 cup water

1 bay leaf

1 teaspoon kosher salt

1 large egg

1 teaspoon cornstarch

2 (5- to 6-ounce) cans tuna, drained

1 cup frozen peas, thawed

2 tablespoons sour cream

1 tablespoon heavy (whipping) cream

1. Sauté the onions and celery. Preheat the Instant Pot® by selecting Sauté and adjust to More for high heat. Heat the oil until it shimmers. Add the onion and celery and cook, stirring frequently, until softened, about 1 minute.

2. Pressure cook. Add the noodles, ¾ cup of evaporated milk, water, bay leaf, and salt to the pot. Stir to combine and submerge the noodles in the liquid. Lock the lid into place. Select Manual; adjust the pressure to Low and the time to 5 minutes. After cooking, quick release the pressure. Unlock and remove the lid.

3. Finish the dish. In a small bowl, whisk together the remaining ¾ cup of evaporated milk, the egg, and the cornstarch (you can do this while the noodles cook). Select Sauté and adjust to Less for low heat. Pour the milk mixture into the noodles and cook, stirring, until the sauce has thickened. Add the tuna and peas and stir gently. Let the tuna and peas heat for 1 to 2 minutes, then stir in the sour cream and heavy cream. Serve.

SERVING TIP: If you like a crunchy topping on your casserole, crumble ¼ cup or so of potato chips or buttery crackers over the top of each serving.

PER SERVING Calories: 450; Fat: 22g; Sodium: 772mg; Carbohydrates: 29g; Fiber: 3g; Protein: 35g

SESAME-SOY CHICKEN WINGS (PAGE 153)

CHAPTER 7

POULTRY

Whatever your favorite part of the bird—thighs, drumsticks, breasts, or wings—you'll find recipes here that suit your taste. It's undeniable that thighs are the best cut for a pressure cooker, since they can stand overcooking better than the leaner breast meat. But that's not to say that you can't pressure cook chicken or turkey breast; with care and attention, you'll end up with tender, juicy breast meat. You can even cook a whole bird, should you so desire.

For more tips and techniques on cooking chicken in the Instant Pot®, see The Best Chicken Ever on page 25.

MULLIGATAWNY SOUP

Mulligatawny soup is a British adaptation of an Indian dish that's changed so much from the original it's barely recognizable. It's exceptionally tasty, nonetheless. As large as the number of people making mulligatawny soup is, the number of versions is just as large. In my version, the apple might seem like a strange addition, but it adds a welcome tart note to the spicy soup. **SERVES 4**

PREP AND FINISHING
15 minutes

MANUAL
8 minutes
high pressure

RELEASE
Natural for 5 minutes

**TOTAL TIME
35 MINUTES**

60 MIN OR LESS

ONE POT

2 tablespoons unsalted butter

1 large onion, chopped (about 1½ cups)

2 celery stalks, chopped (about ¾ cup)

2 medium carrots, peeled and chopped (about ¾ cup)

1 garlic clove, minced

1 tablespoon curry powder, or more to taste

½ teaspoon kosher salt

1 pound boneless, skinless chicken thighs

⅓ cup uncooked basmati or long-grain white rice

4 cups Chicken Stock (page 228)

1 large Granny Smith apple, cored, peeled, and chopped (about 1½ cups)

½ teaspoon cayenne pepper (optional)

¼ cup plain Yogurt (page 230)

1 tablespoon chopped fresh cilantro

1. Sauté the vegetables. Preheat the Instant Pot® by selecting Sauté and adjust to Normal for medium heat. Put the butter in the pot to melt. When it has stopped foaming, add the onion, celery, carrots, and garlic and cook, stirring frequently, until the vegetables start to soften, 2 to 3 minutes. Add the curry powder and salt and cook, stirring, until the curry powder is fragrant, about 1 minute.

2. Pressure cook the soup. Add the chicken, rice, and stock. Lock the lid into place. Select Manual; adjust the pressure to High and the time to 8 minutes. After cooking, naturally release the pressure for 5 minutes, then quick release any remaining pressure. Unlock and remove the lid. Transfer the chicken thighs to a plate.

3. **Finish the soup.** Select Sauté and adjust to Less for low heat. Add the apple and simmer until tender, about 5 minutes. Test the rice to make sure it's done, and adjust the seasoning, adding the cayenne (if using) and more curry powder if desired. While the soup simmers, cut the chicken into bite-size pieces. Return it to the soup to warm through. Ladle the soup into bowls, top with a spoonful of yogurt and a sprinkle of cilantro, and serve.

INGREDIENT TIP: If possible, use Madras curry powder, which tends to be a bit spicier and more complex than other powders. If you can't find it, you may wish to add the optional cayenne to bring up the heat level.

PER SERVING Calories: 403; Fat: 15g; Sodium: 735mg; Carbohydrates: 29g; Fiber: 4g; Protein: 37g

PERFECT CHICKEN BREAST
THREE WAYS

Boneless, skinless chicken breasts are among the easiest proteins to cook, but they are also one of the hardest to do properly. Without skin to protect the meat, which is extremely lean, it dries out quickly. You might think this is inevitable; maybe you've resigned yourself to relying on sauces to make up for the lack of moisture and flavor. But all is not lost! It is possible to cook chicken breasts so they're juicy and tender, even in the pressure cooker. What's more, you can cook a variety of delicious sauces at the same time, so dinner is just a few minutes away. **SERVES 4**

PREP AND FINISHING
10 minutes

MANUAL
5 minutes
low pressure

RELEASE
Natural for 8 minutes

**TOTAL TIME
30 MINUTES**

30 MIN OR LESS

ONE POT

GRAIN-FREE

CORE INGREDIENTS
2 (14- to 16-ounce) boneless, skinless chicken breasts

½ teaspoon kosher salt, plus more to taste

FOR CREAMY PESTO SAUCE
⅓ cup heavy (whipping) cream

¼ cup Chicken Stock (page 228)

1 tablespoon dry white wine

4 tablespoons pesto, homemade (see page 87) or prepared, divided

FOR ROMESCO SAUCE
1 large roasted red pepper, puréed (about ½ cup)

⅓ cup strained tomatoes or tomato sauce

¼ cup Chicken Stock (page 228)

1 tablespoon extra-virgin olive oil

½ teaspoon smoked or regular paprika

½ teaspoon kosher salt

¼ teaspoon cayenne pepper

1 teaspoon sherry vinegar or apple cider vinegar

¼ cup toasted slivered almonds

FOR COCONUT-CURRY SAUCE
½ cup coconut milk

¼ cup Chicken Stock (page 228)

1 teaspoon Thai red curry paste

½ teaspoon curry powder

1 tablespoon freshly squeezed lime juice

1 teaspoon sugar

¼ cup roasted unsalted peanuts, crushed

1 tablespoon minced fresh basil

1. **Prepare the chicken.** Season the chicken on both sides with the salt.

2. **Prepare the sauce.**

For Creamy Pesto Sauce: Pour the cream, stock, and wine into the Instant Pot®. Stir in 3 tablespoons of pesto.

For Romesco Sauce: Pour the red pepper purée, tomatoes, stock, and oil into the pot. Add the paprika, salt, and cayenne and stir to combine.

For Coconut-Curry Sauce: Pour the coconut milk and stock into the pot. Add the curry paste and curry powder and stir to combine.

3. Pressure cook. Put the chicken breasts on a trivet or shallow steamer basket and place in the pot. Lock the lid into place. Select Manual; adjust the pressure to Low and the time to 5 minutes. After cooking, naturally release the pressure for 8 minutes, then quick release any remaining pressure. Unlock and remove the lid. Transfer the chicken breasts to a plate or rack. Use a thermometer to check their internal temperature; the breasts should register 150°F in the center.

4. Finish the sauce. Select Sauté and adjust to Normal for medium heat.

For Creamy Pesto Sauce: Simmer until the sauce thickens slightly, 1 to 2 minutes. Stir in the remaining 1 tablespoon of pesto and add more salt if necessary.

For Romesco Sauce: Add the vinegar and simmer until the sauce thickens slightly, 1 to 2 minutes.

For Coconut-Curry Sauce: Add the lime juice and sugar and simmer until the sauce thickens slightly, 1 to 2 minutes.

5. Serve the chicken. While the sauce simmers, slice the chicken against the grain and divide among four plates.

For Creamy Pesto Sauce: Top the chicken with the sauce and serve.

For Romesco Sauce: Top the chicken with the sauce, garnish with the toasted almonds, and serve.

For Coconut-Curry Sauce: Top the chicken with the sauce, garnish with the peanuts and basil, and serve.

PER SERVING Calories: 246; Fat: 3g; Sodium: 436mg; Carbohydrates: 0g; Fiber: 0g; Protein: 52g

PER SERVING (CREAMY PESTO SAUCE VARIATION) Calories: 351; Fat: 13g; Sodium: 584mg; Carbohydrates: 1g; Fiber: 0g; Protein: 54g

PER SERVING (ROMESCO SAUCE VARIATION) Calories: 326; Fat: 10g; Sodium: 881mg; Carbohydrates: 5g; Fiber: 2g; Protein: 54g

PER SERVING (COCONUT-CURRY SAUCE VARIATION) Calories: 380; Fat: 15g; Sodium: 490mg; Carbohydrates: 5g; Fiber: 2g; Protein: 55g

BALSAMIC AND HONEY–GLAZED CHICKEN AND CARROTS

The combination of balsamic vinegar, honey, and mustard makes a fantastic sauce for chicken and carrots—sweet, tangy, and a bit spicy all at once. Braising the chicken thighs under pressure before running them under the broiler yields silky, tender meat with lightly crisp skin. Broiling them does take a few extra minutes, but it's definitely worth the time, as it adds more depth of flavor and texture to the dish. **SERVES 4**

PREP AND FINISHING
20 minutes

MANUAL
10 minutes
high pressure

RELEASE
Natural for 5 minutes

TOTAL TIME
40 MINUTES

60 MIN OR LESS

GRAIN-FREE

DAIRY-FREE

4 to 6 bone-in, skin-on chicken thighs

½ teaspoon kosher salt

2 tablespoons extra-virgin olive oil

3 large carrots, peeled and cut into 1-inch lengths

¼ cup Chicken Stock (page 228)

½ cup balsamic vinegar

2 tablespoons honey

1 tablespoon Dijon-style mustard

½ teaspoon dried thyme or 1 teaspoon fresh thyme leaves

1. Sear the chicken. Sprinkle the chicken thighs on both sides with the salt. Preheat the Instant Pot® by selecting Sauté and adjust to More for high heat. Heat the oil in the pot until it shimmers. Add the chicken thighs, skin-side down, and let them cook, undisturbed, until the skin is dark golden brown and most of the fat under the skin has rendered out, about 5 minutes. Do not crowd the thighs; if necessary, work in batches. Flip the thighs and cook until light golden brown on the other side, about 3 minutes. Transfer the thighs to a plate and set aside.

2. Make the sauce. Carefully pour off almost all the fat, leaving just enough to cover the bottom of the pressure cooker with a thick coat (about 1 tablespoon). Add the carrots and let them cook, undisturbed, until they begin to brown, about 2 minutes. Add the stock and scrape the bottom of the pan to release the browned bits. Add the vinegar, honey, mustard, and thyme and stir to combine. Return the chicken thighs, skin-side up, to the pot.

3. **Pressure cook the chicken.** Lock the lid into place. Select Manual; adjust the pressure to High and the time to 10 minutes. After cooking, naturally release the pressure for 5 minutes, then manually release any remaining pressure. Remove the chicken thighs from the pot and place them, skin-side up, on a rack set over a baking sheet.

4. **Crisp the chicken.** While the pressure releases on the chicken, preheat the broiler. After the chicken has cooked, place the baking sheet and rack with the chicken thighs in the oven on the top or second rack (depending on the strength of your broiler). Broil until browned, 3 to 5 minutes. Continue with the sauce while the chicken crisps.

5. **Finish the dish.** Remove the carrots from the pot. Let the sauce simmer for several minutes until it's reduced to a glaze. To serve, ladle a spoonful of sauce onto each plate and top with a spoonful of carrots and a chicken thigh (this keeps the skin crisper than putting the sauce over the chicken). Serve.

COOKING TIP: You may prefer to sear the chicken thighs in a skillet on the stove rather than in the pressure cooker; if so, follow the directions through deglazing the pan with the stock (step 2), then pour the pan juices into the pot and continue.

PER SERVING Calories: 463; Fat: 21g; Sodium: 522mg; Carbohydrates: 15g; Fiber: 2g; Protein: 52g

THAI CASHEW CHICKEN

If there's one thing I miss about San Francisco, even after all these years, it's my neighborhood Thai restaurants. Not that Atlanta doesn't have good Thai places, but none of them are near me. I have gotten better at cooking my own, though, and this dish is one of my favorites. Crunchy cashews are a great match for the spicy chicken and vegetables. If you prefer milder food, reduce the amount of red pepper flakes or eliminate them entirely. **SERVES 4**

PREP AND FINISHING
20 minutes

MANUAL
5 minutes
high pressure

RELEASE
Natural for 5 minutes

TOTAL TIME
35 MINUTES

60 MIN OR LESS

ONE POT

DAIRY-FREE

¼ cup all-purpose flour

1 teaspoon kosher salt

1 pound boneless, skinless chicken thighs

3 tablespoons vegetable oil

½ cup Chicken Stock (page 228)

2 tablespoons soy sauce

1 tablespoon fish sauce

1 tablespoon freshly squeezed lime juice

2 teaspoons sugar

1 teaspoon red pepper flakes

½ small onion, sliced thin (about ½ cup)

1 small red bell pepper, seeded and cut into 1-inch pieces

1 medium jalapeño, seeded and cut into thin half-moons

2 teaspoons cornstarch

1 tablespoon water

1 cup roasted unsalted cashews

1. Dredge and brown the chicken. Mix the flour and salt in a shallow dish. Dredge the chicken thighs in the flour, lightly coating both sides. Gently shake off any excess flour. Preheat the Instant Pot® by selecting Sauté and adjust to More for high heat. Heat the oil until it shimmers. Add the chicken in a single layer (you may want to do two batches or use a skillet on the stove). Let cook, undisturbed, until golden brown, 4 to 5 minutes. Flip the thighs and cook until browned on the other side, 3 to 4 minutes. Transfer the thighs to a plate and let cool for a few minutes, then cut into bite-size pieces.

2. Prepare the sauce. While the chicken cools, pour any accumulated fat out of the pot. While the pot is still hot, pour in the chicken stock and stir, scraping up any browned bits from the bottom. Simmer the stock until it reduces by about half. Add the soy sauce, fish sauce, lime juice, sugar, and red pepper flakes to the pot and stir to combine.

3. Pressure cook. Add the cut-up chicken, onion, bell pepper, and jalapeño to the pot. Lock the lid into place. Select Manual; adjust the pressure to High and the time to 5 minutes. After cooking, naturally release the pressure for 5 minutes, then quick release any remaining pressure. Unlock and remove the lid.

4. Finish the dish. In a small bowl, whisk together the cornstarch and water until the mixture is smooth. Stir this into the sauce and cook until the sauce thickens, 2 to 3 minutes. Taste and adjust the seasoning, if necessary. Add the cashews and mix gently. Serve.

INGREDIENT TIP: If you can't find unsalted roasted cashews, you can roast your own. Toss 1 cup of raw cashews with 2 teaspoons of oil and spread them out on a baking sheet. Bake in a preheated 350°F oven until the cashews are fragrant and dark golden brown, 5 to 10 minutes.

PER SERVING Calories: 566; Fat: 35g; Sodium: 1580mg; Carbohydrates: 25g; Fiber: 2g; Protein: 40g

ORANGE CHICKEN

If you're a fan of Panda Express's orange chicken, I think you'll like this recipe. While it doesn't have the crispy fried coating of the fast-food version, the chicken has a great texture, and the sauce has tons of flavor. Delicious and healthier to boot! That's something we can all get behind. **SERVES 4**

PREP AND FINISHING
20 minutes

MANUAL
5 minutes
high pressure

RELEASE
Natural for 5 minutes

TOTAL TIME
35 MINUTES

60 MIN OR LESS

ONE POT

DAIRY-FREE

¼ cup all-purpose flour

1 teaspoon kosher salt

1½ pounds boneless, skinless chicken thighs

3 tablespoons vegetable oil

2 teaspoons minced peeled ginger

1 garlic clove, minced

¼ cup Chicken Stock (page 228)

1 teaspoon grated orange zest

¼ cup freshly squeezed orange juice

2 tablespoons soy sauce

1 tablespoon rice vinegar

1 tablespoon orange juice concentrate

1 teaspoon red pepper flakes

3 scallions, sliced, greens and whites separated

2 teaspoons cornstarch

1 tablespoon water

2 teaspoons toasted sesame oil

Steamed rice, for serving

1. Dredge and brown the chicken. Mix the flour and salt in a shallow dish. Dredge the chicken thighs in the flour, lightly coating both sides, and shake off any excess flour. Preheat the Instant Pot® by selecting Sauté and adjust to More for high heat. Heat the oil until it shimmers. Add the chicken in a single layer (you may want to do two batches or use a skillet on the stove). Let cook, undisturbed, until golden brown, 4 to 5 minutes. Flip the chicken and cook until browned on the other side, 3 to 4 minutes. Transfer the chicken to a plate and let cool for a few minutes, then cut into bite-size pieces.

2. Prepare the sauce. While the chicken cools, pour most of the fat out of the pot, leaving a thin coat. With the pot still on Sauté, add the ginger and garlic and cook, stirring, until fragrant, 1 to 2 minutes. Pour in the chicken stock and stir, scraping up any browned bits from the bottom of the pot. Simmer the stock until it reduces by about half. Add the orange zest and juice, soy sauce, rice vinegar, orange juice concentrate, and red pepper flakes and stir to combine.

3. Pressure cook. Add the cut-up chicken and the white parts of the scallions to the Instant Pot®. Lock the lid into place. Select Manual; adjust the pressure to High and the time to 5 minutes. After cooking, naturally release the pressure for 5 minutes, then quick release any remaining pressure. Unlock and remove the lid.

4. Finish the dish. In a small bowl, whisk together the cornstarch and water until the mixture is smooth. Stir this into the sauce and cook until the sauce thickens, 2 to 3 minutes. Taste and adjust the seasoning, if necessary. Drizzle with the sesame oil and top with the green parts of the scallions. Serve over rice.

PER SERVING Calories: 490; Fat: 25g; Sodium: 1229mg; Carbohydrates: 12g; Fiber: 1g; Protein: 51g

MILK-BRAISED CHICKEN
WITH LEMON-GARLIC SAUCE

I must admit that I was dubious about pressure cooking a whole chicken. Most recipes seemed to guarantee dried-out breast meat and rubbery skin. Then I remembered a recipe for roasted chicken in milk, which originated with Jamie Oliver and was popularized by *The Kitchn* website. After a couple of tries, I came up with this recipe. The time might seem way too short for a whole chicken, but it works. Cooking the chicken with the thighs and legs submerged in liquid and the breast facing up results in moist, tender chicken, whether your preference is white or dark meat. **SERVES 4**

PREP AND FINISHING
25 minutes

MANUAL
12 minutes
low pressure

RELEASE
Natural for 8 minutes

**TOTAL TIME
50 MINUTES**

60 MIN OR LESS

GRAIN-FREE

1 (4- to 4½-pound) whole chicken, giblets removed

1 teaspoon kosher salt

2 tablespoons extra-virgin olive oil or vegetable oil

½ cup Chicken Stock (page 228)

1½ cups whole milk

Zest of one lemon (grated or in strips)

10 garlic cloves, peeled

1. Sear the chicken. Sprinkle the chicken all over with the salt. Heat a large, heavy skillet on the stove over medium-high heat. (If you prefer to sear the chicken in the Instant Pot®, preheat it by selecting Sauté and adjust to More, then proceed as follows.) Heat the oil until it shimmers. Blot the chicken dry and place it in the skillet, breast-side down. Let it cook, undisturbed, until the skin is dark golden brown, about 5 minutes. Turn the chicken over and brown the other side, about 5 minutes. Use tongs to turn the chicken on one side for 2 to 3 minutes more, then repeat on the other side. Transfer the chicken to a plate.

2. Make the sauce. Pour off all the fat, but leave the skillet or pot on the heat. Add the stock and scrape the bottom of the pan to release the browned bits. If you're using a skillet, pour the stock and browned bits into the Instant Pot®.

3. Pressure cook the chicken. Pour the milk into the pot. Place the chicken, breast-side up, in the pot and add the zest and garlic. Lock the lid into place. Select Manual; adjust the pressure to Low and the time to 12 minutes. After cooking, naturally release the pressure for 8 minutes, then quick release any remaining pressure. Remove the chicken from the pot and place it on a rack set over a baking sheet. The temperature of the chicken breast should be just under 150°F, with the thigh meat at about 165°F. If the temperature is much lower than that, return the chicken to the pot and put the lid on, but don't lock it. Keep the chicken on warm for a few minutes until it registers the proper temperatures.

4. Finish the dish. Let the chicken rest on the rack while you finish the sauce. If your zest is in strips, remove and discard them. For a smoother sauce, blend it with an immersion blender. Cut the chicken into serving pieces, spoon the sauce over, and serve.

PER SERVING Calories: 558; Fat: 27g; Sodium: 910mg; Carbohydrates: 7g; Fiber: 0g; Protein: 69g

RED CHICKEN ENCHILADAS

If you're like me, your first introduction to enchiladas was at an Americanized Mexican restaurant. But those overstuffed tortillas swimming in a tomato-based sauce and smothered in cheese bear little resemblance to true Mexican enchiladas. In Mexico, enchiladas are all about the tortillas and the chile sauce. Fillings are minimal. In this recipe, I've tried to remain true to the Mexican version, but I also include a cheesy Mexican-American variation. Both are delicious. **SERVES 4**

PREP AND FINISHING
30 minutes

MANUAL
10 minutes
high pressure

RELEASE
Natural for 10 minutes

**TOTAL TIME
50 MINUTES**

60 MIN OR LESS

1 pound boneless, skinless chicken thighs

2 cups Ancho Chile Sauce (page 239)

½ cup chopped onion

12 corn tortillas

3 tablespoons vegetable oil or nonstick cooking spray

½ cup crumbled queso fresco

FOR MEXICAN-AMERICAN-STYLE ENCHILADAS

2 cups shredded Monterey Jack cheese

1. Pressure cook the chicken. Put the chicken thighs in the Instant Pot®. Pour in the ancho chile sauce. Lock the lid into place. Select Manual; adjust the pressure to High and the time to 10 minutes. After cooking, naturally release the pressure for 10 minutes, then quick release any remaining pressure. Unlock and remove the lid. Transfer the chicken to a bowl and let it cool for a few minutes. Keep the sauce warm.

2. Prepare the filling. When the chicken is just cool enough to handle, cut or pull it into bite-size chunks. Mix in about ⅔ cup of the warm sauce; the chicken should be well coated with sauce but not drowning. Put the onion in a small bowl.

3. Prepare the tortillas. Preheat the oven to 350°F. Place 6 tortillas on a baking sheet in a single layer. Brush the tortillas lightly with the oil (or spray with cooking spray), then turn them over and repeat on the other side. Bake just until the tortillas are warm and pliable, about 3 minutes. Remove from the oven and place the tortillas in a stack on a plate. Cover with aluminum foil to keep warm. Repeat with the remaining 6 tortillas. (If you have two baking sheets, you can heat them all at once.) Leave the oven on. ➤

POULTRY

151

4. **Make the enchiladas.** Spoon about ½ cup warm sauce into a 9-by-13-inch baking dish. Place one tortilla in the sauce and flip it so it's lightly coated on both sides, then place a couple of table-spoons of chicken and a couple of teaspoons of chopped onion on the tortilla.

For Mexican-American-Style Enchiladas: Sprinkle a tablespoon of shredded Monterey Jack cheese over the chicken and onion.

5. **Finish the enchiladas.** Roll the tortilla up and place it at the end of the dish, seam-side down. Repeat with the remaining tor-tillas. When all the enchiladas are filled and rolled, pour enough sauce over them to just cover them (they should not be swim-ming in sauce).

For Mexican-American-Style enchiladas: Sprinkle the rest of the shredded Monterey Jack cheese over the enchiladas.

6. **Bake the enchiladas.** Bake until warmed through, 8 to 10 min-utes. Sprinkle the queso fresco over the enchiladas and serve.

PER SERVING Calories: 695; Fat: 38g; Sodium: 1654mg; Carbohydrates: 67g; Fiber: 5g; Protein: 51g

SESAME-SOY CHICKEN WINGS

There's no denying that frying or roasting chicken wings produces wonderful, crispy skin, but it's messy and time consuming. Instead, for velvety meat that practically falls off the bone, try braising your chicken wings in a savory soy-based broth. One taste and you'll forget all about Buffalo wings! **SERVES 4**

PREP AND FINISHING
15 minutes

MANUAL
10 minutes
high pressure

RELEASE
Quick

TOTAL TIME
30 MINUTES

30 MIN OR LESS

ONE POT

DAIRY-FREE

12 whole chicken wings or 24 wing segments (drumettes and/or flats)

1½ cups water, plus more as needed

½ cup soy sauce

2 tablespoons toasted sesame oil

2 or 3 slices peeled ginger

3 garlic cloves, lightly smashed

2 tablespoons sugar

1 teaspoon Chinese five-spice powder

2 tablespoons minced fresh cilantro, basil, or scallion greens, for garnish

1. Prepare the wings. If you have whole wings, cut off the tips and save them to make Chicken Stock (see page 228) or discard. Cut each wing at the joint into a drumette and a flat segment.

2. Pressure cook. Pour the water and soy sauce into the Instant Pot®. Add the sesame oil, ginger, garlic, sugar, and five-spice powder and stir to combine. Add the chicken wings and stir to coat with the liquid. The wings should be mostly submerged; if necessary, add a little more water. Lock the lid into place. Select Manual; adjust the pressure to High and the time to 10 minutes. After cooking, quick release the pressure. Unlock and remove the lid. Using a spider or skimmer, remove the wings from the pot and set aside on a plate.

3. Finish the wings. Select Sauté and adjust to More for high heat. Bring the sauce to a boil and let it reduce by about half. Return the wings to the sauce and stir to coat. Transfer the wings to a deep platter or bowl and pour the sauce over. Garnish with the cilantro and serve.

PER SERVING Calories: 297; Fat: 21g; Sodium: 1797mg; Carbohydrates: 9g; Fiber: 7g; Protein: 18g

CHICKEN TINGA

If you like chicken cooked in salsa as a taco filling, wait until you taste this Mexican classic! With not much more effort than opening a jar of salsa, you can have tender chicken simmered in a complex tomatillo and tomato sauce flavored with garlic and herbs. Serve the chicken in tortillas or taco shells or over tostadas, garnished with avocado slices or crumbled mild cheese, for a simple, delicious dinner. **SERVES 4**

PREP AND FINISHING
15 minutes

MANUAL
10 minutes
high pressure

RELEASE
Natural for 10 minutes

**TOTAL TIME
40 MINUTES**

2 tablespoons extra-virgin olive oil

8 ounces tomatillos (2 to 3 large), husked and quartered

1 medium onion, chopped (about 1 cup)

2 garlic cloves, minced

½ cup Chicken Stock (page 228)

1 (14-ounce) can fire-roasted tomatoes, undrained

1 teaspoon dried oregano

½ teaspoon kosher salt, plus more to taste

¼ teaspoon ground cumin

1 pound boneless, skinless chicken thighs

1 teaspoon chipotle purée (see page 22)

60 MIN OR LESS

ONE POT

GRAIN-FREE

DAIRY-FREE

1. Brown the vegetables. Preheat the Instant Pot® by selecting Sauté and adjust to More for high heat. Heat the olive oil until it shimmers. Add the tomatillos in a single layer and cook, undisturbed, until browned, about 2 minutes. Add the onion and garlic and cook, stirring occasionally, until the onion is browned, about 4 minutes.

2. Prepare the sauce. Add the chicken stock and stir, scraping the bottom of the pot to get up any browned bits. Add the tomatoes with their juice, oregano, salt, and cumin. Stir to combine.

3. **Pressure cook.** Add the chicken to the pot. Lock the lid into place. Select Manual; adjust the pressure to High and the time to 10 minutes. After cooking, naturally release the pressure for 10 minutes, then quick release any remaining pressure. Transfer the chicken to a plate and let cool. When it's cool enough to handle, chop or pull the chicken into bite-size pieces.

4. **Finish the dish.** Use an immersion blender to purée the sauce. (Alternatively, you can purée the sauce in a countertop blender, then return it to the pot.) Stir in the chipotle purée. Select Sauté and adjust to Normal for medium heat. Simmer until the sauce has thickened to the consistency of gravy. Taste and adjust the seasoning, adding more salt if necessary. Add the chicken to the sauce and stir to warm it through. Serve.

PER SERVING Calories: 328; Fat: 16g; Sodium: 491mg; Carbohydrates: 11g; Fiber: 3g; Protein: 35g

CHICKEN CACCIATORE

Mushrooms and tomatoes are the backbone of the traditional cacciatore (hunter's) sauce; red wine and capers add a hint of acidity, making for an easy and delicious sauce for chicken thighs or drumsticks. Chicken cacciatore usually simmers for hours, but you can pressure cook it in a fraction of the time, with no loss of flavor. It's sure to become a family favorite. **SERVES 4**

PREP AND FINISHING
20 minutes

MANUAL
10 minutes
high pressure

RELEASE
Natural for 10 minutes

**TOTAL TIME
45 MINUTES**

60 MIN OR LESS

ONE POT

GRAIN-FREE

DAIRY-FREE

4 to 6 bone-in, skin-on chicken thighs and/or drumsticks

½ teaspoon kosher salt, plus more to taste

2 tablespoons extra-virgin olive oil

1 small onion, sliced

2 garlic cloves, minced

8 ounces cremini or white button mushrooms, cleaned and sliced

⅓ cup dry red wine

½ cup Chicken Stock (page 228)

1 (14-ounce) can diced tomatoes, undrained

1 teaspoon dried oregano

2 tablespoons chopped fresh parsley

2 tablespoons drained capers

1. Sear the chicken. Sprinkle the chicken pieces on both sides with the salt. Preheat the Instant Pot® by selecting Sauté and adjust to More for high heat. Heat the oil until it shimmers. Add the chicken, skin-side down, and cook, undisturbed, until the skin is dark golden brown and most of the fat under the skin has rendered out, about 5 minutes. Do not crowd; work in batches if necessary. Flip the chicken and cook until light golden brown on the other side, about 3 minutes. Transfer the chicken to a plate.

2. Make the sauce. Carefully pour off almost all the fat, leaving just enough to cover the bottom of the pot with a thick coat (about 1 tablespoon). Add the onion and garlic and cook, stirring frequently, until the onion begins to brown, about 3 minutes. Add the mushrooms and cook until they begin to soften, 1 to 2 minutes. Add the wine and scrape the bottom of the pot to release the browned bits. Boil until the liquid reduces by about half. Add the stock, tomatoes with their juice, and oregano. Add the chicken pieces, skin-side up, to the pot.

3. **Pressure cook.** Lock the lid into place. Select Manual; adjust the pressure to High and the time to 10 minutes. After cooking, naturally release the pressure for 10 minutes, then quick release any remaining pressure. Transfer the chicken to a plate.

4. **Finish the dish.** Strain the sauce into a fat separator and let it rest until the fat rises to the surface. (If you don't have a fat separator, let the sauce sit for a few minutes, then spoon or blot off any excess fat from the top of the sauce.) Pour the defatted sauce back into the pot and select Keep Warm. If you prefer a thicker sauce, select Sauté and adjust to Less. Let the sauce simmer for several minutes until it's reduced to the consistency you like. Adjust the seasoning, adding more salt if necessary, and stir in the parsley and capers. Serve the chicken topped with the sauce.

PER SERVING Calories: 456; Fat: 21g; Sodium: 676mg; Carbohydrates: 10g; Fiber: 3g; Protein: 51g

CHICKEN AND BISCUITS

I think of this dish as the oven version of chicken and dumplings. In my house dumplings were always made from a light baking powder dough and steamed on top of the chicken and vegetables. The biscuit recipe here is so easy you can make it while the chicken cooks. To save even more time, bake them separately while the chicken pressure cooks, then serve the biscuits topped with the chicken, or place a biscuit on top of a bowl of savory chicken and vegetables. **SERVES 4**

PREP AND FINISHING
30 minutes

MANUAL
5 minutes
high pressure

RELEASE
Quick

TOTAL TIME
40 MINUTES

60 MIN OR LESS

¼ cup all-purpose flour

½ teaspoon kosher salt

⅛ teaspoon freshly ground black pepper

⅛ teaspoon cayenne pepper

1¼ pounds boneless, skinless chicken thighs

¼ cup unsalted butter

3 cups Chicken Stock (page 228)

3 large carrots, peeled and cut into 1-inch lengths

2 large celery stalks, cut into ½-inch slices

1 cup frozen pearl onions

1 bay leaf

⅔ cup frozen peas, thawed

FOR THE BISCUITS
1½ cups self-rising flour

¾ cup heavy (whipping) cream

1. Dredge and brown the chicken. Mix the flour, salt, black pepper, and cayenne pepper in a shallow dish. Dredge the chicken thighs in the flour, lightly coating both sides. Gently shake off any excess flour. Reserve the flour to use again in step 2. Preheat the Instant Pot® by selecting Sauté and adjust to More for high heat. Put the butter in the pot to melt. When it has stopped foaming, add the chicken in a single layer (you may need to do two batches). Cook, undisturbed, until golden brown, 4 to 5 minutes. Flip the chicken and cook until browned on the other side, 3 to 4 minutes. Transfer the chicken to a plate and let cool for a few minutes, then cut into bite-size pieces.

2. Prepare the sauce. With the pot still on Sauté, add the remaining flour mixture to the butter in the pot. Cook, stirring constantly, until the roux (a smooth, paste-like mixture) is golden brown. Add about 1 cup of the stock, whisking until it is combined with the roux. Add the rest of the stock and stir, scraping up any browned bits from the bottom of the pot, until the sauce has thickened slightly. If the sauce is very thick, add more chicken stock until the sauce is the consistency of a light gravy.

3. Pressure cook. Add the cut-up chicken, carrots, celery, pearl onions, and bay leaf to the pot. Lock the lid into place. Select Manual; adjust the pressure to High and the time to 5 minutes. After cooking, quick release the pressure. Unlock and remove the lid. Add the thawed peas and stir to warm them through.

4. Make the biscuits. While the chicken cooks, preheat the oven to 400°F. In a medium bowl, whisk the flour and cream until the mixture holds together.

5. Finish the dish. Spoon the chicken mixture into a shallow baking dish. Scoop the biscuit dough into balls about 1½ inches in diameter and place evenly over the chicken mixture. Bake until the biscuits are golden brown, 12 to 14 minutes. Remove the bay leaf and serve.

PER SERVING Calories: 707; Fat: 31g; Sodium: 1135mg; Carbohydrates: 54g; Fiber: 5g; Protein: 50g

PARMESAN TURKEY MEATBALLS

Parmesan cheese, garlic, and parsley flavor these easy turkey meatballs. They cook in a very plain tomato sauce, which lets the flavor of the meatballs themselves shine through, but feel free to use a more complex homemade or commercial sauce if you like. **SERVES 4**

PREP AND FINISHING
15 minutes

MANUAL
5 minutes
high pressure

RELEASE
Natural for 5 minutes

**TOTAL TIME
30 MINUTES**

30 MIN OR LESS

ONE POT

1 pound ground turkey

½ medium onion, finely chopped

3 garlic cloves, minced

2 tablespoons minced fresh parsley

½ cup grated Parmesan or similar cheese

½ teaspoon kosher salt

1 large egg

2 tablespoons whole milk

¼ cup bread crumbs

2 tablespoons extra-virgin olive oil

½ cup Chicken Stock (page 228)

1 (14-ounce) can diced tomatoes, undrained

1. Make the meatballs. In a large bowl, gently mix the ground turkey, onion, garlic, parsley, Parmesan cheese, and salt. In a small bowl, whisk together the egg and milk. Stir in the bread crumbs. Add the egg-crumb mixture to the meat and gently mix together until just evenly combined. Form meatballs using about 2 tablespoons of meat for each. You may find it easier to roll the balls if you moisten your hands with water.

2. Brown the meatballs. Preheat the Instant Pot® by selecting Sauté and adjust to More for high heat. Heat the oil until it shimmers. Add the meatballs in a single layer and let them cook, undisturbed, until browned on the bottom, 1 to 2 minutes. Turn the meatballs to brown on the opposite side. Move the meatballs to the sides of the pot (they may stack on top of each other) and pour in the chicken stock. Bring the liquid to a boil and scrape up any browned bits from the bottom of the pot. Add the tomatoes with their juice and move the meatballs back into an even layer. ➤

3. **Pressure cook.** Lock the lid into place. Select Manual; adjust the pressure to High and the time to 5 minutes. After cooking, naturally release the pressure for 5 minutes, then quick release any remaining pressure. Unlock and remove the lid.

4. **Finish the sauce.** Use a slotted spoon to transfer the meatballs to a bowl. Select Sauté and adjust to More for high heat. Bring the sauce to a boil and cook until it is very thick and chunky. Spoon the sauce over the meatballs and serve.

PREP TIP: Recipes for meatballs seem to fall into two camps: those that are browned before cooking in sauce, and those that go into the sauce naked, so to speak. These bridge the gap, with two sides browned, which gives the meatballs some structure and provides more flavor but is not nearly as time consuming as browning all the sides. If you like, turn the meatballs several times to brown all the sides.

PER SERVING Calories: 404; Fat: 25g; Sodium: 714mg; Carbohydrates: 12g; Fiber: 2g; Protein: 40g

HONEY MUSTARD–GARLIC WINGS

For years, I've said that my mother invented honey mustard. Long before the grocery stores groaned with rows of commercial honey mustard, she was combining those two condiments for what was back then a wildly exotic sauce. Add some garlic, and you've got the perfect glaze for chicken wings. Starting them in the pressure cooker and finishing them under the broiler gives you the best of both worlds—tender meat and crisp skin. It doesn't get better than that. **SERVES 4**

PREP AND FINISHING
15 minutes

MANUAL
10 minutes
high pressure

RELEASE
Quick

**TOTAL TIME
30 MINUTES**

30 MIN OR LESS

GRAIN-FREE

DAIRY-FREE

12 whole chicken wings or 24 wing segments (drumettes and/or flats)

1 cup water, for steaming

⅓ cup honey

⅓ cup Dijon-style mustard

4 garlic cloves, minced

1. Prepare the wings. If you have whole wings, cut off the tips and save them to make Chicken Stock (see page 228) or discard. Cut each wing at the joint into a drumette and a flat segment.

2. Pressure cook. Place the chicken wings in a steamer basket. Pour the water into the Instant Pot® and place the basket in the pot. Lock the lid into place. Select Manual; adjust the pressure to High and the time to 10 minutes. After cooking, quick release the pressure. Unlock and remove the lid. Remove the wings from the pot and transfer them to a rack set over a baking sheet.

3. Finish the wings. Preheat the broiler. In a small bowl, mix the honey, mustard, and garlic. Baste the wings with about half of the sauce. Broil the wings until browned, 4 to 6 minutes. Flip the wings and baste them with the remaining sauce. Broil until the second side is browned, 3 to 6 minutes. Serve.

PER SERVING Calories: 351; Fat: 18g; Sodium: 66mg; Carbohydrates: 29g; Fiber: 2g; Protein: 20g

CAJUN-SPICED TURKEY BREAST

The first time I hosted Thanksgiving dinner, I went with a menu from *Gourmet* magazine for a Cajun-inspired meal. One of the best parts was the turkey, which benefited from a spiced butter rubbed under the breast skin, keeping the meat moist and adding tons of flavor. I've long since lost the rest of the menu, but I go back to that preparation any time I want to cook a turkey breast. In the Instant Pot®, you won't get the crisp skin of the oven version, but the butter will flavor the meat and keep it succulent and tender. **SERVES 4**

PREP AND FINISHING
15 minutes

MANUAL
20 minutes
low pressure

RELEASE
Natural for 10 minutes

**TOTAL TIME
50 MINUTES**

60 MIN OR LESS

ONE POT

1 teaspoon kosher salt, plus more to taste

½ teaspoon freshly ground black pepper, plus more to taste

½ teaspoon dried basil

½ teaspoon dried thyme

½ teaspoon granulated garlic

¼ teaspoon cayenne pepper

4 tablespoons unsalted butter, at room temperature

1 small (about 5 pounds) whole turkey breast

1 cup Chicken Stock (page 228)

2 tablespoons cornstarch

2 tablespoons water

1. Prepare the turkey. In a small bowl, add the salt, black pepper, basil, thyme, garlic, cayenne pepper, and butter and mix the herbs and spices into the butter. Use your hands to loosen the skin over the turkey breast and spread the spiced butter under the skin as evenly as possible.

2. Pressure cook. Pour the stock into the Instant Pot®. Place the breast in the pot. Lock the lid into place. Select Manual; adjust the pressure to Low and the time to 20 minutes. After cooking, naturally release the pressure for 10 minutes, then quick release any remaining pressure. Unlock and remove the lid. Transfer the turkey to a plate. Use a thermometer to check the temperature; the thickest part of the meat should register 150°F.

3. **Finish the sauce.** In a small bowl, combine the cornstarch and water until the mixture is smooth. Select Sauté and adjust to Normal for medium heat. Bring the chicken stock to a simmer and add the cornstarch mixture. Cook until the gravy has thickened. Taste and adjust the seasoning, adding more salt and black pepper if necessary.

4. **Serve the turkey.** While the gravy simmers, remove the skin from the turkey. Cut the breast into ¼-inch-thick slices and spoon the gravy over them. Serve.

PER SERVING Calories: 275; Fat: 13g; Sodium: 855mg; Carbohydrates: 4g; Fiber: 0g; Protein: 34g

TURKEY TENDERLOINS
WITH LEMON-CAPER SAUCE

Turkey tenderloins, like boneless chicken breasts, need careful treatment, but a quick stint under low pressure with a short resting time produces moist, delicious turkey. Cooking the sauce at the same time means that in just over half an hour, you can have an elegant entrée any night of the week. **SERVES 4**

PREP AND FINISHING
10 minutes

MANUAL
8 minutes
low pressure

RELEASE
Natural for 8 minutes

**TOTAL TIME
35 MINUTES**

60 MIN OR LESS

ONE POT

GRAIN-FREE

2 (14-ounce) turkey tenderloins

½ teaspoon kosher salt

¼ teaspoon freshly ground black pepper

½ cup Chicken Stock (page 228)

3 tablespoons unsalted butter, divided

1 teaspoon grated lemon zest

1 tablespoon freshly squeezed lemon juice

1 tablespoon drained capers

1. Prepare the turkey. Sprinkle the tenderloins on both sides with the salt and pepper.

2. Pressure cook. Pour the chicken stock into the Instant Pot® and add 1 tablespoon of butter. Place the tenderloins in the pot. Lock the lid into place. Select Manual; adjust the pressure to Low and the time to 8 minutes. After cooking, naturally release the pressure for 8 minutes, then quick release any remaining pressure. Unlock and remove the lid. Transfer the tenderloins to a plate. Use a thermometer to check the temperature; the tenderloins should register 150°F in the center.

3. Finish the sauce. Select Sauté and adjust to Normal for medium heat. Bring the sauce to a simmer and add the lemon zest and juice. Cook until the liquid has reduced by about half. Turn off the heat. One tablespoon at a time, whisk in the remaining 2 tablespoons of butter. Stir in the capers.

4. Serve the turkey. While the sauce simmers, slice the turkey against the grain and divide among four plates. Top with the sauce and serve.

PER SERVING Calories: 298; Fat: 10g; Sodium: 603mg; Carbohydrates: 1g; Fiber: 0g; Protein: 48g

CHICKEN AND ORZO
WITH LEMON SAUCE

Based on the classic Greek soup avgolemono, this pasta and chicken dish is as quick to prepare as it is delicious to eat. The lemony sauce is thickened with egg, resulting in a dish that's somewhere between stew and soup. Cooking the chicken breasts whole keeps them moist and tender. The flavor is light and delicious, making it perfect for dinner on a warm spring or summer day. **SERVES 4**

PREP AND FINISHING
15 minutes

MANUAL
4 minutes
low pressure

RELEASE
Natural for 5 minutes

TOTAL TIME
30 MINUTES

30 MIN OR LESS

ONE POT

DAIRY-FREE

4 cups Chicken Stock (page 228), or more as necessary

6 ounces orzo

2 large boneless, skinless chicken breasts

¼ teaspoon kosher salt, plus more to taste

1 large egg

2 tablespoons freshly squeezed lemon juice

Freshly ground black pepper

1. Pressure cook. Pour the stock into the Instant Pot® and stir in the orzo. Place the chicken breasts on top of the orzo and sprinkle them with the salt. Lock the lid into place. Select Manual; adjust the pressure to Low and the time to 4 minutes. After cooking, naturally release the pressure for 5 minutes, then quick release any remaining pressure. Unlock and remove the lid.

2. Finish the chicken. Transfer the chicken breasts to a plate or cutting board and set aside to cool for a minute, then cut into bite-size pieces. Don't worry if the center of the chicken isn't quite done; it will cook again.

3. Finish the dish. Thoroughly beat the egg in a small bowl. Whisk in the lemon juice. Select Sauté on the Instant Pot® and adjust to Normal for medium heat. Slowly add about 1 cup of the warm chicken stock to the egg and lemon mixture, whisking constantly. (If there is not enough stock in the pot to ladle out 1 cup, add more stock and bring it to a simmer.) Add the chicken pieces and simmer for 1 to 2 minutes, or until the chicken is cooked. Turn off the heat, and add the egg-and-stock mixture to the pot. Stir to combine. Adjust the seasoning if necessary, and serve.

PER SERVING Calories: 310; Fat: 8g; Sodium: 834mg; Carbohydrates: 32g; Fiber: 2g; Protein: 32g

BRAZILIAN CHICKEN THIGHS
WITH DARK BEER

This is another recipe based on one from Jay Harlow's *Beer Cuisine*; I simplified the ingredients list slightly and used all chicken thighs instead of a whole, cut-up chicken. The flavors are fabulous, with the dark beer turning into a sweet and spicy sauce for the succulent chicken. This is comfort food at its finest, especially on a cold day with the winds howling outside your window. Steamed rice and Refried Black Beans (page 80) make good accompaniments. **SERVES 4**

PREP AND FINISHING
20 minutes

MANUAL
10 minutes
high pressure

RELEASE
Natural for 10 minutes

TOTAL TIME
45 MINUTES

60 MIN OR LESS

DAIRY-FREE

4 to 6 bone-in, skin-on chicken thighs

½ teaspoon kosher salt, plus more to taste

2 tablespoons extra-virgin olive oil

1 large onion, sliced

3 large garlic cloves, minced

1 cup dark beer, such as a porter or stout

¼ cup Chicken Stock (page 228)

1 teaspoon smoked or regular paprika

½ teaspoon dried oregano

½ teaspoon dried basil

½ teaspoon red pepper flakes

¼ teaspoon freshly ground black pepper, plus more to taste

1. Sear the chicken. Sprinkle the chicken thighs on both sides with the salt. Heat a large, heavy skillet on the stove over medium-high heat. Heat the oil until it shimmers. (If you prefer to sear the pork in the Instant Pot®, preheat the pot by selecting Sauté and adjust to More. Heat the oil until it shimmers.) Add the chicken thighs, skin-side down, and let them cook, undisturbed, until the skin is dark golden brown and most of the fat under the skin has rendered out, about 5 minutes. Do not crowd the thighs; if necessary, work in batches. Flip the thighs and cook until light golden brown on the other side, about 3 minutes. Transfer the thighs to a plate.

2. Make the sauce. Carefully pour off almost all the fat, leaving just enough to cover the bottom of the skillet or pot with a thick coat (about 1 tablespoon). Add the onion and garlic and cook, stirring frequently, until the onion begins to brown, about 3 minutes. Add the beer and scrape the bottom of the pan to release the browned bits. Boil until the liquid reduces by about half, about 2 minutes. Add the stock, paprika, oregano, basil, red pepper flakes, and black pepper. Bring the sauce to a boil and cook for 1 minute. If you're using a skillet, pour the sauce into the Instant Pot®. Add the chicken thighs, skin-side up, to the pot.

3. Pressure cook. Lock the lid into place. Select Manual; adjust the pressure to High and the time to 10 minutes. After cooking, naturally release the pressure for 10 minutes, then quick release any remaining pressure. Remove the chicken thighs and place them on a rack set over a baking sheet. Let the chicken rest on the rack while you finish the sauce.

4. Finish the dish. Strain the sauce into a fat separator and let it rest until the fat rises to the surface. (If you don't have a fat separator, let the sauce sit for a few minutes, then spoon or blot off any excess fat from the top of the sauce.) Pour the defatted sauce back into the Instant Pot® and select Keep Warm. If you prefer a thicker sauce, select Sauté and adjust to Less. Let the sauce simmer for several minutes until it's reduced to the consistency you like. Adjust the seasoning, adding more salt and black pepper if needed. Serve the chicken thighs topped with the sauce.

PER SERVING Calories: 434; Fat: 20g; Sodium: 493mg; Carbohydrates: 6g; Fiber: 1g; Protein: 51g

RED WINE–BRAISED SHORT RIBS (PAGE 188)

CHAPTER 8
MEAT

Tougher cuts of meat, like chuck roast, pork shoulder, ribs, or lamb shanks, benefit most from pressure cooking. But with care, it's also possible to cook leaner, more tender cuts like pork tenderloin or sirloin steak. You'll find recipes for both types of cuts in this chapter. Because meat doesn't brown while cooking under pressure, most of the recipes here start by searing the meat. In dishes that call for cubed meat, like stew or chili, I prefer to sear the meat before cutting it. Because the Instant Pot® is deep and narrow, not much evaporation occurs while searing, so lots of little pieces of meat tend to steam rather than brown. It's easier to sear one big piece—and you get even tastier results.

SOUTHWESTERN PORK AND HOMINY STEW
(POZOLE VERDE)

I grew up eating hominy occasionally, but it always came from a can. When I finally tasted it made from scratch, I realized why pozole is such a popular dish. Until I got a pressure cooker, though, I never would have cooked it—3 to 4 hours simmering was not a commitment I was willing to make. Fortunately, the Instant Pot® makes pozole as quick as it is delicious. **SERVES 4**

PREP AND FINISHING
20 minutes

MANUAL
30 minutes
high pressure

RELEASE
Natural for 10 minutes

**TOTAL TIME
1 HOUR
10 MINUTES,
PLUS OVERNIGHT
TO SOAK**

ONE POT

DAIRY-FREE

8 ounces dried hominy (pozole)

1½ pounds boneless country-style pork ribs, trimmed of excess fat

1½ teaspoons kosher salt, divided, plus more to taste

2 tablespoons vegetable oil

1 small onion, sliced (about 1 cup)

2 garlic cloves, minced

½ cup mild beer, such as a lager or pale ale

1 pound tomatillos, husked and diced (about 2 cups)

¼ cup canned diced green chiles, drained

1 medium jalapeño, seeded and chopped

¼ teaspoon ground cumin

4 cups Chicken Stock (page 228)

1 avocado, peeled, pitted, and chopped

2 tablespoons chopped fresh cilantro

1. Soak the hominy. In a large bowl, cover the dried hominy by about 2 inches of water. Soak at room temperature for 8 to 24 hours. Drain and rinse, then drain again.

2. Brown the pork. Sprinkle the ribs on both sides with ½ teaspoon of salt. Preheat the Instant Pot® by selecting Sauté and adjust to More for high heat. Heat the oil until it shimmers. Add the ribs in a single layer and cook, undisturbed, until browned, about 3 minutes. Flip the ribs and repeat on the second side. Transfer the ribs to a plate.

3. Brown the onion. Add the onion and garlic and cook, stirring occasionally, until starting to brown, about 3 minutes. Add the beer and cook, scraping up any browned bits from the bottom of the pot. Let the beer simmer until it has reduced by about half.

4. Pressure cook. Add the tomatillos, green chiles, jalapeño, cumin, remaining 1 teaspoon of salt, and stock to the pot. Add the hominy to the pot along with the browned ribs. Lock the lid into place. Select Manual; adjust the pressure to High and the time to 30 minutes. After cooking, naturally release the pressure for 10 minutes, then quick release any remaining pressure. Unlock and remove the lid.

5. Finish the stew. Remove the pork from the stew and shred it with two forks, discarding any fat or gristle. Return the meat to the pot. Blot or skim any fat from the surface of the stew. Taste and adjust the seasoning, adding more salt if necessary. Ladle the stew into bowls, top with the avocado and cilantro, and serve.

INGREDIENT TIP: This stew is a great opportunity for using the leftover liquid from Carnitas (page 176). Measure it out and add enough chicken stock to make 4 cups. Taste it and adjust the salt accordingly.

PER SERVING Calories: 525; Fat: 25g; Sodium: 1919mg; Carbohydrates: 25g; Fiber: 8g; Protein: 49g

FARFALLE
WITH ITALIAN SAUSAGE AND PEPPERS

Whether you call them farfalle, butterflies, or bowties, this pasta is one of my favorites. It catches just the right amount of sauce and pairs well with bite-size pieces of meat and vegetables. Here, I match farfalle with spicy Italian sausage and peppers for a classically delicious, one-pot pasta dinner. **SERVES 4**

PREP AND FINISHING
10 minutes

MANUAL
12 minutes
high pressure
+ 4 minutes
low pressure

RELEASE
Natural for
10 minutes + Quick

**TOTAL TIME
45 MINUTES**

60 MIN OR LESS

ONE POT

DAIRY-FREE

2 tablespoons extra-virgin olive oil

1 pound hot Italian sausage, casings removed, cut into 1-inch pieces

½ medium onion, sliced (about ½ cup)

¼ cup dry white wine

1½ cups strained tomatoes or tomato sauce

¾ teaspoon kosher salt, divided

8 ounces farfalle pasta

1 medium red or green bell pepper, seeded and chopped

1¼ cups water

1. Start the sauce. Preheat the Instant Pot® by selecting Sauté and adjust to More for high heat. Heat the oil until it shimmers. Add the sausage in a single layer. Brown the sausage pieces on all sides, about 3 minutes, then push the meat to the sides of the pot. Add the onion and cook, stirring, until the onion pieces separate and begin to soften, 2 to 3 minutes. Add the wine and stir, scraping the bottom of the pot to dissolve the browned bits. Pour in the tomatoes, add ¼ teaspoon of salt, and stir to combine.

2. Pressure cook the sauce. Lock the lid into place. Select Manual; adjust the pressure to High and the time to 12 minutes. After cooking, naturally release the pressure for 10 minutes, then quick release any remaining pressure. Unlock and remove the lid.

3. Pressure cook the pasta. Add the pasta, bell pepper, water, and remaining ½ teaspoon of salt. Stir to combine. Lock the lid into place. Select Manual; adjust the pressure to Low and the time to 4 minutes. After cooking, quick release the pressure. Unlock and remove the lid. Test the pasta; it should be tender with just a slightly firm center. If it's not done enough, simmer for 1 to 2 minutes until it is done to your liking. Stir and serve.

PER SERVING Calories: 657; Fat: 41g; Sodium: 1786mg; Carbohydrates: 40g; Fiber: 2g; Protein: 30g

SMOKY-SWEET SPARE RIBS

When I first read about glazing meat with the combination of hoisin and chipotles, I was intrigued. I regularly use both those ingredients but had never thought of mixing them in the same recipe. It turns out to be a match made in heaven. You get the heat and smokiness of the chipotle, plus the sweet-salty punch of hoisin. It's fusion food in the best sense of the term. **SERVES 4**

PREP AND FINISHING
15 minutes

MANUAL
20 minutes
high pressure

RELEASE
Natural for 15 minutes

**TOTAL TIME
55 MINUTES**

60 MIN OR LESS

DAIRY-FREE

1 rack spare ribs (about 3 pounds)

1 teaspoon kosher salt

1 cup water, for steaming

½ cup hoisin sauce

2 to 3 tablespoons chipotle purée (see page 22)

1. Prepare the ribs. Sprinkle the ribs on both sides with the salt. Cut the rack into three pieces. If desired, remove the membrane from the bone side of the ribs, or cut through it every couple of inches.

2. Pressure cook. Pour the water into the Instant Pot®. Place a trivet in the pot and place the ribs on top, stacking them if necessary. Lock the lid into place. Select Manual; adjust the pressure to High and the time to 20 minutes. After cooking, naturally release the pressure for 15 minutes, then quick release any remaining pressure. Unlock and remove the lid. Use tongs to transfer the ribs, bone-side up, to a rack set over a baking sheet, or to a broiler pan.

3. Finish the ribs. Preheat the broiler and move the oven rack to the highest position. In a small bowl, whisk together the hoisin sauce and chipotle purée. Baste the bone side of the rib sections with about half of the sauce and place under the broiler until browned and bubbling, 3 to 5 minutes. Turn the ribs over, baste the other side, and broil them for another 3 to 5 minutes. Serve.

COOKING TIP: If you prefer, you can grill the ribs rather than broiling them. Prepare a medium-hot charcoal fire, or heat a gas grill to medium. Baste as directed and grill the ribs until browned and crusty, 3 to 4 minutes per side.

PER SERVING Calories: 314; Fat: 7g; Sodium: 1195mg; Carbohydrates: 14g; Fiber: 1g; Protein: 46g

MEAT

CARNITAS

Carnitas is one of my all-time favorite taco fillings. The succulent pork chunks with their crispy edges need only a sprinkling of chopped onions and jalapeños, with a squirt of fresh lime or a spoonful of salsa. Unlike Pork Shoulder (page 185), carnitas is cooked first in a flavorful liquid, then browned in the hot fat that remains after cooking. Made the traditional way, it takes hours, but with the initial cooking done under pressure, it'll be ready in about an hour. **SERVES 4**

PREP AND FINISHING
20 minutes

MANUAL
25 minutes
high pressure

RELEASE
Natural for 10 minutes

TOTAL TIME
1 HOUR

60 MIN OR LESS

GRAIN-FREE

DAIRY-FREE

2½ pounds bone-in country-style pork ribs (or 2 pounds if boneless)

1 teaspoon kosher salt

¼ cup freshly squeezed orange juice

¼ cup Chicken Stock (page 228)

½ medium onion, cut into eighths

3 garlic cloves, coarsely chopped

1 to 3 tablespoons bacon fat, lard, or vegetable oil

1. **Prepare the ribs.** Sprinkle the ribs on both sides with the salt.

2. **Pressure cook.** Pour the orange juice and stock into the Instant Pot® and add the onion and garlic. Place the ribs in the pot, arranging them in a single layer. Select Manual; adjust the pressure to High and the time to 25 minutes. After cooking, naturally release the pressure for 10 minutes, then quick release any remaining pressure. Unlock and remove the lid. Use tongs to transfer the ribs to a plate.

3. **Prepare the pork for frying.** Pour the accumulated liquid from the pot into a fat separator and set aside. When the pork is cool enough to handle, pull it into 1-inch chunks, discarding any gristle or fat.

4. Finish the carnitas. When the fat has risen to the top of the fat separator, pour off the liquid, leaving just the fat. (If desired, save the liquid for another use, such as the Southwestern Pork and Hominy Stew on page 172.) Pour the fat into a large cast iron or other heavy skillet. Turn the heat to medium and bring the fat to a simmer. Cook until any remaining water has evaporated, leaving just the fat. You should have a thick coating of fat; add enough of the bacon fat to get a depth of about ⅛ inch. Turn the heat up to medium-high. When the fat is shimmering, add the pork chunks in a single layer. Let them brown, undisturbed, until mostly crisp and browned, 2 to 4 minutes. Turn over the pork and brown at least one more side. Serve.

SERVING TIP: Serve the carnitas on warmed corn or flour tortillas with chopped red onion, jalapeño, cilantro, and lime wedges, or your preferred toppings.

PER SERVING Calories: 512; Fat: 20g; Sodium: 792mg; Carbohydrates: 4g; Fiber: 0g; Protein: 74g

PORK TENDERLOIN
WITH CABBAGE AND NOODLES

The beauty of cooking a pork tenderloin in a pressure cooker is that it cooks so quickly that you can pair it with noodles or vegetables, since they'll be done in the same amount of time. The classic German or Eastern European dish of cabbage and noodles makes a delicious and filling accompaniment. **SERVES 4**

PREP AND FINISHING
20 minutes

MANUAL
4 minutes
low pressure

RELEASE
Quick

TOTAL TIME
30 MINUTES

30 MIN OR LESS

ONE POT

DAIRY-FREE

3 bacon slices, chopped

1 medium pork tenderloin (about 1¼ pounds)

1½ teaspoons kosher salt, divided, plus more to taste

¼ teaspoon freshly ground black pepper, plus more to taste

1 teaspoon smoked or regular paprika

1 small onion, sliced (about 1 cup)

½ very small green cabbage, shredded (3 to 4 cups)

⅓ cup dry white wine

1¼ cups Chicken Stock (page 228)

4 ounces wide egg noodles

1. Sauté the bacon. Preheat the Instant Pot® by selecting Sauté and adjust to Normal for medium heat. Cook the bacon until most of the fat has rendered and the bacon is crisp, about 6 minutes. Use a slotted spoon to remove the bacon, and drain on paper towels, leaving the rendered fat in the pot.

2. Sear the pork. Cut the tenderloin in half crosswise. Sprinkle the halves with 1 teaspoon of salt, the pepper, and the paprika. (You can do this while the bacon browns.) With the rendered fat in the pot, select Sauté and adjust to More for high heat. When the fat is hot, add the two pieces of pork tenderloin and sear, undisturbed, until browned, 2 to 3 minutes, then turn and sear the other sides. Transfer to a plate.

3. Sauté the vegetables. Add the onion and cabbage to the pot and stir to coat with the remaining fat. Cook, stirring frequently, until the vegetables start to soften, about 2 minutes. Add the wine and bring to a simmer, scraping up any browned bits from the bottom of the pot. Let the wine reduce slightly.

4. Pressure cook. Add the chicken stock and noodles and stir to cover the noodles with the liquid (add more stock if the noodles are not submerged). Place the pork tenderloin halves on top of the vegetables and noodles. Lock the lid into place. Select Manual; adjust the pressure to Low and the time to 4 minutes. After cooking, quick release the pressure. Unlock and remove the lid.

5. Finish the dish. Check the temperature of the pork; it should be about 145°F. If it is much lower than that, put it back with the noodles and put the lid on but don't lock it into place. Check it again in a couple of minutes. When it's done, transfer the pork to a cutting board and let it rest for a couple of minutes. Taste the noodles and cabbage and adjust the seasoning, adding more salt and pepper if necessary, then spoon into a serving dish. Slice the pork and serve with the cabbage and noodles.

PER SERVING Calories: 406; Fat: 15g; Sodium: 1699mg; Carbohydrates: 15g; Fiber: 3g; Protein: 48g

PORK LOIN BRAISED IN MILK

Like a whole chicken, pork loin takes extremely well to braising in milk, so well that it's easy to see how this became an Italian classic. Although the milk curdles slightly during cooking, you can purée it to make a unique, savory sauce for the tender, moist pork. Best of all, it's done in under an hour. **SERVES 4**

PREP AND FINISHING
25 minutes

MANUAL
10 minutes
low pressure

RELEASE
Natural for 12 minutes

TOTAL TIME
55 MINUTES

60 MIN OR LESS

GRAIN-FREE

1 (2- to 2½-pound) pork loin

1 teaspoon kosher salt

½ teaspoon freshly ground black pepper

2 tablespoons vegetable oil

⅓ cup Chicken Stock (page 228)

2 cups whole milk

¼ cup heavy (whipping) cream

½ teaspoon dried sage

3 small onions, quartered

2 large garlic cloves, peeled

2 tablespoons chopped fresh parsley

1. Sear the pork. Sprinkle the pork all over with the salt and pepper. Heat a large, heavy skillet on the stove over medium-high heat. Heat the oil until it shimmers. (If you prefer to sear the pork in the Instant Pot®, preheat the pot by selecting Sauté and adjust to More. Heat the oil until it shimmers.) Add the pork to the skillet, fat-side down. Let it cook, undisturbed, until the fat side is golden brown, about 4 minutes. Flip the pork and brown the other side for 3 minutes. Turn and brown the sides for about 2 minutes each. Transfer the pork to a plate.

2. Deglaze the pan. Pour off all the fat, but leave the skillet or pot on the heat. Pour in the chicken stock and scrape the bottom of the pan to release the browned bits. If you're using a skillet, pour the stock and browned bits into the pot.

3. Pressure cook. Pour the milk and cream into the Instant Pot®. Stir in the sage. Add the pork, fat-side up, and the onion quarters and garlic cloves. Lock the lid into place. Select Manual; adjust the pressure to Low and the time to 10 minutes. After cooking, naturally release the pressure for 12 minutes, then manually release any remaining pressure. Unlock and remove the lid.

4. Braise the pork. Check the temperature of the center of the pork. It should read between 110°F and 115°F. Select Sauté and adjust to Less for low heat. Bring the sauce to a simmer and cook the pork in the sauce for 3 to 5 minutes. Flip the pork and simmer for another 2 to 3 minutes, then check the temperature again. You're looking for a temperature of about 145°F in the center of the pork. Simmer a little longer if necessary until it reaches the correct temperature.

5. Finish the dish. Transfer the pork to a cutting board and allow it to rest for several minutes. Finish the sauce by blending it until smooth with an immersion blender. Slice the pork and place it on a serving platter. Spoon the sauce over the slices, sprinkle with the parsley, and serve.

PER SERVING Calories: 883; Fat: 53g; Sodium: 877mg; Carbohydrates: 14g; Fiber: 2g; Protein: 83g

SMOTHERED PORK CHOPS

Like the Pork Loin Braised in Milk (page 180), pork loin chops need very little time in the pressure cooker, lest they become overcooked. But with a little care, you can turn out beautifully browned, tender chops—and make a creamy, delicious sauce at the same time. This is a great meal to serve for a stay-at-home date night or when you have guests. **SERVES 4**

PREP AND FINISHING
20 minutes

MANUAL
1 minute
low pressure

RELEASE
Natural for 4 minutes

**TOTAL TIME
30 MINUTES**

30 MIN OR LESS

4 boneless pork loin chops, about 1½ inches thick

1½ teaspoons kosher salt, divided, plus more to taste

2 tablespoons vegetable oil

1 large onion, sliced thin (about 1½ cups)

8 ounces white button or cremini mushrooms, sliced

½ teaspoon dried thyme

¼ teaspoon freshly ground black pepper, plus more to taste

½ cup dry white wine

1 cup Chicken Stock (page 228)

2 teaspoons Worcestershire sauce

1 tablespoon all-purpose flour

2 tablespoons sour cream

1. Sear the pork loin. Sprinkle the pork chops on both sides with 1 teaspoon of salt. Heat a large, heavy skillet on the stove over medium-high heat. (If you prefer to sear the pork in the Instant Pot®, preheat the pot by selecting Sauté and adjust to More.) Heat the oil until it shimmers. Add the chops and let them cook, undisturbed, until golden brown, about 3 minutes. Flip the chops and brown the other side for 3 minutes. Transfer the chops to a plate.

2. Sauté the vegetables. Add the onion to the skillet or pot and cook, stirring frequently, until the onion pieces start to separate and soften, 2 to 3 minutes. Add the mushrooms and sprinkle with the remaining ½ teaspoon of salt, the thyme, and the black pepper. Cook, stirring occasionally, until the mushrooms are soft and starting to brown, 2 to 3 minutes.

3. **Deglaze the pan**. Add the wine and scrape the bottom of the pan to release the browned bits. Let the wine simmer until reduced by about half. If you're using a skillet, transfer the mushrooms and onions with the liquid to the pot.

4. **Pressure cook**. In a medium bowl, whisk together the chicken stock, Worcestershire sauce, and flour. Add to the Instant Pot® and stir to combine with the onions and mushrooms. Transfer the chops to the pot and spoon some of the onion mixture over them. Lock the lid into place. Select Manual; adjust the pressure to Low and the time to 1 minute. After cooking, naturally release the pressure for 4 minutes, then quick release any remaining pressure. Unlock and remove the lid.

5. **Finish the dish**. Transfer the pork chops to a serving platter. Add the sour cream to the sauce and stir to combine. Taste and adjust the seasoning, adding more salt or pepper if necessary. Spoon the sauce over the chops and serve.

PER SERVING Calories: 336; Fat: 13g; Sodium: 1180mg; Carbohydrates: 8g; Fiber: 1g; Protein: 40g

PORK SHOULDER
THREE WAYS

Once you get this simple technique down for cooking pork shoulder, you can keep it plain or dress it up in all kinds of ways. The three sauces I include travel from Jamaica to New Orleans to Singapore for a delicious variety that will please every palate. While you can use a single piece of pork shoulder for this dish, I prefer country-style ribs, which are boneless strips of shoulder. They cook faster and more evenly. If you do get a shoulder roast, I recommend cutting it into pieces about 2 inches thick. **SERVES 4**

PREP AND FINISHING
20 minutes

MANUAL
25 minutes
high pressure

RELEASE
Natural for 10 minutes

TOTAL TIME
1 HOUR

60 MIN OR LESS

ONE POT

DAIRY-FREE

CORE INGREDIENTS

2½ pounds boneless country-style pork ribs

1½ teaspoons kosher salt, plus more to taste

2 tablespoons vegetable oil

½ cup Chicken Stock (page 228)

FOR JERK SAUCE

½ cup mild beer, such as a lager or pale ale

2 tablespoons sherry vinegar

1 habanero chile, seeded and minced

2 garlic cloves, minced

2 tablespoons grated peeled ginger

2 tablespoons brown sugar

2 teaspoons ground allspice

1½ teaspoons kosher salt

1 teaspoon dried thyme

½ teaspoon ground cinnamon

FOR CAJUN SAUCE

1 (14-ounce) can diced tomatoes, undrained

2 tablespoons apple cider vinegar

1 tablespoon Worcestershire sauce

1 teaspoon Hot Pepper Sauce (page 240)

1 teaspoon smoked or regular paprika

1 teaspoon kosher salt

½ teaspoon freshly ground black pepper

½ teaspoon freshly ground white pepper

½ teaspoon cayenne pepper

½ teaspoon dried basil

½ teaspoon dried thyme

FOR GINGER-SOY SAUCE

½ cup soy sauce

2 tablespoons toasted sesame oil

3 garlic cloves, minced

2 tablespoons grated peeled ginger

2 tablespoons granulated sugar

1 teaspoon Chinese five-spice powder ➤

SERVING TIP: While the pork shoulder is delicious on its own or served over rice, all three versions also make delicious pulled pork sandwiches. Shred the pork rather than leaving it in chunks, and use just enough of the sauce to moisten it. Serve on split hamburger buns.

PER SERVING Calories: 465; Fat: 17g; Sodium: 1129mg; Carbohydrates: 0g; Fiber: 0g; Protein: 74g

PER SERVING (JERK SAUCE VARIATION) Calories: 515; Fat: 17g; Sodium: 2006mg; Carbohydrates: 9g; Fiber: 1g; Protein: 75g

PER SERVING (CAJUN SAUCE VARIATION) Calories: 494; Fat: 17g; Sodium: 1758mg; Carbohydrates: 6g; Fiber: 2g; Protein: 74g

PER SERVING (GINGER-SOY SAUCE VARIATION) Calories: 579; Fat: 24g; Sodium: 2927mg; Carbohydrates: 11g; Fiber: 1g; Protein: 77g

1. **Brown the pork.** Sprinkle the pork with the salt. Preheat the Instant Pot® by selecting Sauté and adjust to More for high heat. Heat the oil until it shimmers. Add the pork in a single layer and cook, undisturbed, until browned, about 3 minutes. Flip the meat and repeat on the other side. Transfer the pork to a plate. Pour the chicken stock into the pot and stir, scraping up any browned bits from the bottom of the pot.

2. **Make the sauce.** In a small bowl, stir together all the ingredients for your choice of sauce.

3. **Pressure cook.** Add the sauce along with the browned pork to the Instant Pot®. Lock the lid into place. Select Manual; adjust the pressure to High and the time to 25 minutes. After cooking, naturally release the pressure for 10 minutes, then quick release any remaining pressure. Unlock and remove the lid.

4. **Finish the dish.** Transfer the pork to a plate or cutting board and cut it into chunks, discarding any fat or gristle. Pour the sauce into a fat separator and let it rest until the fat rises to the surface. Pour the sauce back into the pot. (If you don't have a fat separator, let the sauce sit for a few minutes, then spoon or blot off any excess fat from the top of the sauce, then return the sauce to the pot.) Select Sauté and adjust to More for high heat. Bring the sauce to a boil and cook until it has thickened to a gravy consistency, about 5 minutes. Taste and adjust the seasoning, adding more salt if necessary. Return the pork to the pot and simmer it in the sauce for a few minutes to warm through. Serve.

BARBECUED BEEF SANDWICHES

There's something about tender beef coated with tangy barbecue sauce that's irresistible. Once you have the barbecue sauce made, this recipe is a cinch to cook, with very little hands-on work. Although the sauce is moderately spicy to start with, it loses much of its kick while the meat braises. Rather than cook the beef in all of the sauce, I like to keep a little of the sauce out and add it just to warm through at the end. It gives the sandwiches more punch. **SERVES 4**

PREP AND FINISHING
15 minutes

MANUAL
25 minutes
high pressure

RELEASE
Natural for 15 minutes

TOTAL TIME
1 HOUR

60 MIN OR LESS

ONE POT

DAIRY-FREE

1 (2¼-pound) boneless beef chuck roast

½ teaspoon kosher salt, plus more to taste

2 cups Smoky Barbecue Sauce (page 238), divided

4 hoagie rolls or large hamburger buns, split

1. Prepare the beef. If the chuck roast is more than about 2½ inches thick, cut it into slices about 2 inches thick. Cut off any large chunks of fat. Sprinkle it all over with the salt.

2. Pressure cook. Put the beef in the Instant Pot® and pour 1½ cups of barbecue sauce over it. Lock the lid into place. Select Manual; adjust the pressure to High and the time to 25 minutes. After cooking, naturally release the pressure for 15 minutes, then quick release any remaining pressure. Unlock and remove the lid and transfer the beef to a plate or baking sheet.

3. Finish the sauce. Pour the liquid into a fat separator and allow the fat to rise to the surface, then return the sauce to the pot. (If you don't have a fat separator, spoon or blot off as much fat as possible.) Select Sauté and adjust to Normal for medium heat. Bring the sauce to a boil and let cook until reduced by about half—it should be the original consistency of the barbecue sauce.

4. Shred the beef. While the sauce reduces, shred the beef into small chunks, discarding any fat or gristle.

5. Assemble the sandwiches. Add the shredded beef and the remaining ½ cup of sauce to the pot. Cook, stirring, until the meat heats through. Taste and adjust the seasoning, adding more salt if necessary. Spoon the beef onto the bottom halves of the rolls and top with the remaining halves. Serve.

PER SERVING Calories: 1174; Fat: 79g; Sodium: 1812mg; Carbohydrates: 39g; Fiber: 3g; Protein: 73g

MEAT

RED WINE–BRAISED SHORT RIBS

If there's a better cut of beef to cook in a pressure cooker than short ribs, I don't know what it is. A stint in the Instant Pot® turns these tough ribs into meat so tender that it falls off the bone, but stays succulent and flavorful. The braising liquid turns into an easy red wine sauce for the perfect finishing touch. Serve with the horseradish-garlic variation of Easiest Mashed Potatoes (see the tip on page 59) for a truly hearty meal. **SERVES 4**

PREP AND FINISHING
25 minutes

MANUAL
40 minutes
high pressure

RELEASE
Natural for 20 minutes

TOTAL TIME
1 HOUR 30 MINUTES

GRAIN-FREE

ONE POT

DAIRY-FREE

Kosher salt

8 (2-inch) bone-in beef short ribs (about 4 pounds)

2 tablespoons extra-virgin olive oil, plus additional if needed

2 small carrots, peeled and cut into ¼-inch rounds

1 medium onion, diced

1 garlic clove, minced

1 tablespoon tomato paste

½ cup dry red wine

1 cup low-sodium beef broth

2 fresh thyme sprigs or 1 teaspoon dried thyme

1 bay leaf

Freshly ground black pepper

1 teaspoon brown sugar (optional)

1. Sear the ribs. Liberally salt the short ribs on all sides. Preheat the Instant Pot® by selecting Sauté and adjust to More for high heat. Heat the oil until it shimmers. Add the short ribs in a single layer without crowding them (work in batches if necessary). Brown the ribs for 3 to 4 minutes on each side, then transfer to a plate and set aside, leaving the cooker on high heat.

2. Cook the vegetables. Add another coat of oil if the pan is dry and heat it until shimmering. Add the carrots, onion, and garlic. Sprinkle with ½ teaspoon of salt and stir until the onion pieces separate and the vegetables begin to soften, 2 to 3 minutes.

3. Make the sauce. Stir in the tomato paste and cook for a few minutes, just until the paste begins to brown slightly. Add the wine and stir, scraping the bottom of the pot to dissolve the browned bits. Bring the liquid to a boil and cook until the wine has reduced by about a third, 2 to 3 minutes. Add the beef broth, thyme, and bay leaf. Add the ribs; the meat should be partially but not completely submerged in liquid.

4. **Pressure cook the short ribs.** Lock the lid into place. Select Manual (or Meat); adjust the pressure to High and the time to 40 minutes. After cooking, naturally release the pressure for 20 minutes, then quick release any remaining pressure. Unlock and remove the lid. Carefully transfer the ribs to a plate or baking sheet. They'll be quite tender and will fall off the bones if you're not gentle. Tent lightly with aluminum foil to keep them warm while you finish the sauce.

5. **Finish the sauce.** Strain the sauce mixture through a coarse strainer into a fat separator and discard the solids. When the fat has separated, pour the sauce back into the pot. (If you don't have a fat separator, strain the sauce and let it cool until any fat has risen to the top. Remove as much fat as possible with a spoon or use paper towels to blot it off, then return the sauce to the pot.) Select Sauté and adjust the heat to Normal. Bring the sauce to a simmer, stirring frequently to prevent it from scorching, until the sauce is the consistency of gravy, 8 to 10 minutes. Season with black pepper and taste. If the sauce is too acidic, add the brown sugar. Add more salt if necessary.

6. **Finish the dish.** Return the ribs to the pot and heat them for a minute or two. Serve and garnish, if desired, with a few additional sprigs of fresh thyme on each plate.

INGREDIENT TIP: Frozen pearl onions (thawed) and cooked mushrooms make a great addition to this dish. Add them when you return the strained sauce to the pot.

PER SERVING Calories: 582; Fat: 28g; Sodium: 359mg; Carbohydrates: 7g; Fiber: 2g; Protein: 67g

CHILI CON CARNE

In my first pressure cooker cookbook, I included a recipe for chili with beef and pinto beans. It's really good, but this time around, I wanted to give you a version with no beans. I like to serve this chili with beans on the side so those who want beans can add them. If you like that option, the Cowboy Pinto Beans (page 78) make a great side dish. **SERVES 4**

(page 78)

PREP AND FINISHING
20 minutes

MANUAL
25 minutes
high pressure

RELEASE
Natural for 10 minutes

TOTAL TIME
1 HOUR

60 MIN OR LESS

ONE POT

DAIRY-FREE

1 (2½-pound) boneless beef chuck roast

1 teaspoon kosher salt

2 tablespoons vegetable oil

1 medium onion, chopped (about 1 cup)

2 garlic cloves, minced

1 tablespoon ancho chile powder or similar

1 teaspoon ground cumin

½ teaspoon cayenne pepper

½ teaspoon dried oregano

½ cup mild beer, such as a lager or pale ale

½ cup low-sodium beef broth

½ cup Ancho Chile Sauce (page 239)

2 tablespoons strained tomatoes or tomato sauce

1 teaspoon chipotle purée (see page 22)

1. Sear the beef. Cut the chuck roast into "steaks" about 1½ inches thick. Sprinkle them with the salt. Preheat the Instant Pot® by selecting Sauté and adjust to More for high heat. Heat the oil until it shimmers. (You may find it easier to sear the beef in a heavy skillet on the stove.) Add the beef in a single layer without crowding (work in batches if necessary). Brown the beef for 3 minutes, then turn it over and brown the other side for 3 minutes. Transfer the beef to a plate or cutting board and set aside to cool slightly, then cut into 1-inch cubes.

2. Cook the onion and garlic. Leaving the pot on high heat, add the onion and garlic. Cook, stirring occasionally, until the onion begins to brown, about 3 minutes. Add the chile powder, cumin, cayenne, and oregano and cook, stirring frequently, until fragrant, about 1 minute.

3. Make the sauce. Add the beer and stir, scraping the bottom of the pot to dissolve the browned bits. Bring to a boil and cook until the beer has reduced by about a third, 1 to 2 minutes. (If you're using a skillet, pour the beer and browned bits into the Instant Pot®.) Add the beef broth, ancho chile sauce, strained tomatoes, and chipotle purée and stir to combine.

4. Pressure cook. Add the beef cubes and any accumulated juices to the pot. Lock the lid into place. Select Manual; adjust the pressure to High and the time to 25 minutes. After cooking, naturally release the pressure for 10 minutes, then quick release any remaining pressure. Serve.

INGREDIENT TIP: Searing the beef in "steaks" and then cubing it, rather than cutting and then searing, is not only quicker but also results in better browning. This is because cubes of beef release so much liquid that they tend to steam in the deep pot rather than brown.

PER SERVING Calories: 1122; Fat: 86g; Sodium: 904mg; Carbohydrates: 5g; Fiber: 1g; Protein: 75g

QUICK BEEF STEW

Like the Chili con Carne recipe (page 190), this one starts with searing chuck steaks and mushrooms to form the base for a savory cooking sauce. Cooking the stew in two stages ensures fork-tender beef with a bounty of perfectly done vegetables, all in under an hour. A side salad and biscuits or crusty bread are all you need for an easy weeknight meal. **SERVES 4**

PREP AND FINISHING
15 minutes

MANUAL
20 + 4 minutes
high pressure

RELEASE
Quick

**TOTAL TIME
45 MINUTES**

60 MIN OR LESS

ONE POT

DAIRY-FREE

1 (2-pound) boneless beef chuck roast

1 teaspoon kosher salt, plus more to taste

2 tablespoons vegetable oil

8 ounces white button or cremini mushrooms, quartered

½ cup dry red wine

2½ cups low-sodium beef broth

1 tablespoon all-purpose flour

1 small onion, quartered

3 medium garlic cloves, peeled

2 bay leaves

¼ teaspoon freshly ground black pepper, plus more to taste

1 pound small red potatoes, quartered

2 medium carrots, peeled and cut into 1-inch pieces

1 cup frozen pearl onions

1 cup frozen peas, thawed

1. Sear the beef. Cut the chuck roast into "steaks" about 1½ inches thick. Sprinkle them on both sides with the salt. Preheat the Instant Pot® by selecting Sauté and adjust to More for high heat. Heat the oil until it shimmers. (You may find it easier to sear the beef in a heavy skillet on the stove.) Add the beef in a single layer without crowding it (work in batches if necessary). Brown the beef for 3 minutes, then turn it over and brown the other side. Transfer the beef to a plate or cutting board and set aside to cool slightly, then cut into 1-inch cubes.

2. Cook the mushrooms. Leaving the pot on high heat, add the mushrooms. Cook, stirring occasionally, until they are mostly golden brown, 3 to 5 minutes. Transfer to a bowl and set aside.

3. Make the sauce. Add the wine and stir, scraping the bottom of the pot to dissolve the browned bits. Bring the liquid to a boil and cook until the wine has reduced by about a third, 1 to 2 minutes. (If you're using a skillet, pour the wine and browned bits into the Instant Pot®.) In a medium bowl, whisk together the beef broth and flour. Add it to the pot, along with the onion quarters, garlic cloves, and bay leaves. Stir to combine.

4. Pressure cook the beef. Add the beef cubes with any accumulated juices to the pot. Lock the lid into place. Select Manual; adjust the pressure to High and the time to 20 minutes. After cooking, quick release the pressure. Unlock and remove the lid.

5. Pressure cook the stew. Remove and discard the onion quarters, garlic cloves (if they haven't dissolved), and bay leaves. Add the black pepper, potatoes, carrots, and frozen pearl onions to the pot. Lock the lid into place. Select Manual; adjust the pressure to High and the time to 4 minutes. After cooking, quick release the pressure. Unlock and remove the lid.

6. Finish the stew. If you prefer a thicker sauce, let the stew simmer for several minutes, until thickened to your taste. Add the peas and reserved mushrooms and cook just until heated through. Taste and adjust the seasoning, adding more salt and pepper if necessary. Serve.

PER SERVING Calories: 1085; Fat: 71g; Sodium: 698mg; Carbohydrates: 37g; Fiber: 8g; Protein: 68g

ITALIAN POT ROAST

I based the braising liquid in this delicious recipe on one I use in my pork Italiano (Philadelphia's other iconic sandwich, in case you didn't know). It works equally well with beef, and this pot roast makes a tasty change from the usual version. Try the leftovers warmed in a sandwich, with a slice or two of provolone cheese melted on top. **SERVES 6**

PREP AND FINISHING
20 minutes

MANUAL
40 + 4 minutes
high pressure

RELEASE
Quick

TOTAL TIME
1 HOUR 15 MINUTES

GRAIN-FREE

DAIRY-FREE

1 (3- to 3½-pound) boneless chuck roast, about 3 inches thick

1½ teaspoons kosher salt

2 tablespoons vegetable oil

1 cup dry red wine

¾ cup low-sodium beef broth

1 teaspoon fennel seeds

1 teaspoon dried thyme

¾ teaspoon red pepper flakes

¼ teaspoon freshly ground black pepper

1 bay leaf

1 fresh rosemary sprig

1 fresh parsley sprig

1 small onion, quartered

2 large garlic cloves, lightly smashed

1 pound red potatoes, scrubbed and quartered

2 carrots, peeled and cut into 1-inch pieces

2 celery stalks, cut into ½-inch slices

1 medium red bell pepper, seeded and cut into 1½-inch chunks

1. Sear the beef. Sprinkle the beef on both sides with the salt. Heat a large, heavy skillet on the stove over medium-high heat. Heat the oil until it shimmers. (If you prefer to sear the roast in the Instant Pot®, preheat the pot by selecting Sauté and adjust to More. Heat the oil until it shimmers.) Blot the roast dry with paper towels and add it to the skillet. Let it cook, undisturbed, until deeply browned, about 3 minutes. Flip the roast and brown the other side for 3 minutes. Transfer the beef to a plate.

2. Make the sauce. Pour off the oil from the pan. Pour in the wine and stir, scraping the bottom of the pan to dissolve the browned bits. Bring the wine to a boil and cook until reduced by about half, 1 to 2 minutes. If you're using a skillet, pour the wine and browned bits into the Instant Pot®. Add the beef broth, fennel seeds, thyme, red pepper flakes, black pepper, bay leaf, rosemary, parsley, onion, and garlic. Stir to combine.

3. Pressure cook the beef. Add the beef with any accumulated juices to the pot. Lock the lid into place. Select Manual; adjust the pressure to High and the time to 40 minutes. After cooking, quick release the pressure. Unlock and remove the lid.

4. Pressure cook the vegetables. Transfer the beef to a cutting board and tent with a piece of aluminum foil. Remove and discard the bay leaf, rosemary sprig, and parsley sprig. Add the potatoes, carrots, celery, and bell pepper to the pot. Lock the lid into place. Select Manual; adjust the pressure to High and the time to 4 minutes. After cooking, quick release the pressure. Unlock and remove the lid.

5. Finish the dish. While the vegetables are cooking, cut the beef against the grain into slices about ⅓ inch thick. Transfer them to a serving platter. When the vegetables are done, spoon them and the sauce over the beef and serve.

INGREDIENT TIP: When you buy a beef chuck pot roast, you may end up with a small chunk of it being more fibrous and tough than the rest of the cut. That's because chuck, or beef shoulder, is a collection of five or more muscles. The muscle that attaches to the neck has more connective tissue than the others, and depending on where in the shoulder your cut comes from, you may end up with a piece of it. Don't worry; sliced thin and trimmed of the connective tissue, it's very tasty, but you'll find it doesn't shred like the rest of the shoulder.

PER SERVING Calories: 1113; Fat: 78g; Sodium: 875mg; Carbohydrates: 19g; Fiber: 3g; Protein: 72g

SOUTHWESTERN POT ROAST

For a spectacular twist on traditional pot roast, try this southwestern version, spiced up with charred onions and garlic and three kinds of chiles. It's got tons of flavor but only very mild heat, so it's great for the whole family. I prefer a thinner sauce with pot roast rather than a true gravy. If you like a thicker sauce, stir in 1 tablespoon of all-purpose flour mixed with 1 tablespoon of water after the vegetables are cooked. Simmer for a few minutes to cook off the raw flour taste and thicken the sauce. **SERVES 6**

PREP AND FINISHING
25 minutes

MANUAL
40 + 4 minutes
high pressure

RELEASE
Quick

TOTAL TIME
1 HOUR 25 MINUTES

DAIRY-FREE

1 (3- to 3½-pound) boneless chuck roast, about 3 inches thick

1½ teaspoons kosher salt

2 tablespoons vegetable oil

1 medium onion, quartered

3 large garlic cloves, lightly smashed

¾ cup mild beer, such as a lager or pale ale

¾ cup low-sodium beef broth

2 tablespoons Ancho Chile Sauce (page 239)

¼ cup canned diced green chiles, drained

1 teaspoon ground cumin

1 teaspoon dried oregano

1 pound red potatoes, quartered

1 medium red bell pepper, seeded and cut into 1½-inch chunks

1 medium green bell pepper, seeded and cut into 1½-inch chunks

1 large jalapeño, seeded and cut into half-moons

1. Sear the beef. Sprinkle the beef on all sides with the salt. Heat a large, heavy skillet on the stove over medium-high heat. Heat the oil until it shimmers. (If you prefer to sear the roast in the Instant Pot®, preheat the pot by selecting Sauté and adjust to More. Heat the oil until it shimmers.) Blot the roast dry with paper towels and add it to the skillet. Let it cook, undisturbed, until deeply browned, about 3 minutes. Flip the roast and brown the other side for 3 minutes. Transfer the beef to a plate.

2. Brown the onion and garlic. Leaving the skillet or pot on high heat, add the onion quarters and garlic cloves. Cook, without stirring, until the first side is darkly browned, even charred a bit, 2 to 3 minutes. Turn the onion and garlic over and repeat on the other side. Transfer to the plate with the beef.

3. **Make the sauce.** Pour off the oil from the pan. Pour in the beer and stir, scraping the bottom of the pan to dissolve the browned bits. Bring the beer to a boil and cook until reduced by about a third, 1 to 2 minutes. If you're using a skillet, pour the beer and browned bits into the Instant Pot®. Add the beef broth, ancho chile sauce, green chiles, cumin, and oregano. Stir to combine.

4. **Pressure cook the beef.** Add the beef with any accumulated juices, onion quarters, and garlic to the pot. Lock the lid into place. Select Manual; adjust the pressure to High and the time to 40 minutes. After cooking, quick release the pressure. Unlock and remove the lid.

5. **Pressure cook the vegetables.** Transfer the beef to a cutting board and tent with a piece of aluminum foil. Add the potatoes, bell peppers, and jalapeño to the pot. Lock the lid into place. Select Manual; adjust the pressure to High and the time to 4 minutes. After cooking, quick release the pressure. Unlock and remove the lid.

6. **Finish the dish.** While the vegetables are cooking, cut the beef against the grain into slices about ⅓ inch thick. Transfer them to a serving platter. When the vegetables are done, spoon them and the sauce over the beef and serve.

PER SERVING Calories: 1094; Fat: 79g; Sodium: 509mg; Carbohydrates: 19g; Fiber: 3g; Protein: 72g

ITALIAN-STYLE LAMB SHANKS
WITH WHITE BEANS

Lamb shanks and beans are kind of a production, but they're so fabulous together they're worth it for a special weekend dinner or a dinner party. I love the very mild and subtle licorice flavor of fennel with lamb, but if you don't, or you can't find fennel, feel free to leave it out. If you do, you may want to garnish the dish with a sprinkle of fresh parsley. **SERVES 4**

PREP AND FINISHING
25 minutes

MANUAL
35 + 10 minutes
high pressure

RELEASE
Natural for
10 + 10 minutes

TOTAL TIME
1 HOUR
35 MINUTES,
PLUS OVERNIGHT
TO SOAK

ONE POT

GRAIN-FREE

DAIRY-FREE

1 tablespoon plus 2 teaspoons kosher salt, divided

1 quart water

8 ounces dried cannellini or white northern beans

4 (10-ounce) lamb shanks

2 tablespoons extra-virgin olive oil

½ cup dry white wine or dry white vermouth

1 bay leaf

1 medium onion, quartered

2 garlic cloves, minced

2 large carrots, peeled, 1 quartered and 1 coarsely chopped

1 small fennel bulb, quartered, fronds reserved (optional)

2 cups Chicken Stock (page 228), plus additional if needed

1 medium tomato, seeded and chopped

Freshly ground black pepper

1. Soak the beans. In a large bowl, dissolve 1 tablespoon of salt in the water. Add the beans and soak at room temperature for 8 to 24 hours. Rinse and drain.

2. Prep the lamb. Sprinkle the lamb shanks with 1½ teaspoons of salt. Cover with aluminum foil and let them sit at room temperature for 20 minutes to 2 hours. The longer they sit, the better. If they sit for 1 hour or less, it can be at room temperature. If they sit for longer than 1 hour, let them do so in the refrigerator.

3. Brown the lamb. Preheat the Instant Pot® by selecting Sauté and adjust to More for high heat. Heat the oil until it shimmers. Blot the lamb shanks dry with a paper towel. Add two shanks to the pot and cook, undisturbed, until browned, about 5 minutes. Turn over and repeat on the second side. Transfer the shanks to a plate and repeat with the remaining two shanks, transferring them to the plate when browned. Add the wine and cook, scraping to get up any browned bits from the bottom of the pot. Simmer the wine until it reduces by about half. ➤

4. **Pressure cook the lamb.** Add the bay leaf, onion, garlic, quartered carrot, and fennel (if using) to the pot. Transfer the browned shanks to the pot and pour in the stock. Lock the lid into place. Select Manual; adjust the pressure to High and the time to 35 minutes. After cooking, naturally release the pressure for 10 minutes, then quick release any remaining pressure. Unlock and remove the lid.

5. **Strain the sauce.** Transfer the shanks to a plate. Strain the sauce into a fat separator or bowl, discarding the vegetables. Let the fat rise for 5 minutes or so and then pour the sauce back into the pot, spooning off as much fat as possible if the sauce is in a bowl.

6. **Pressure cook the beans.** Add the beans to the pot along with the chopped carrot and tomato. Make sure that the beans are covered by about an inch of liquid. If they are not, add more stock. Return the lamb to the pot. Lock the lid into place. Select Manual; adjust the pressure to High and the time to 10 minutes. After cooking, naturally release the pressure for 10 minutes, then quick release any remaining pressure. Unlock and remove the lid.

7. **Finish the dish.** Taste and adjust the seasoning, adding more salt if necessary and seasoning with black pepper. If the beans are too soupy, select Sauté and adjust to Normal for medium heat. Simmer until the sauce thickens slightly. Serve the beans in bowls, each topped with a lamb shank and sprinkled with the fennel fronds (if using).

PREPARATION TIP: Salting the lamb ahead of time not only seasons it but also intensifies the flavor. You can even salt the shanks when you start soaking the beans; overnight is not too long.

PER SERVING Calories: 753; Fat: 24g; Sodium: 1829mg; Carbohydrates: 46g; Fiber: 18g; Protein: 85g

BEEF VINDALOO

Another British version of an Indian classic, beef vindaloo is a deliciously spicy stew-like entrée. I like to serve it with plenty of rice and some steamed vegetables to temper the heat of the cayenne. **SERVES 4**

PREP AND FINISHING
15 minutes

MANUAL
25 minutes
high pressure

RELEASE
Natural for 15 minutes

**TOTAL TIME
1 HOUR**

60 MIN OR LESS

ONE POT

DAIRY-FREE

PER SERVING Calories: 970; Fat: 70g; Sodium: 825mg; Carbohydrates: 5g; Fiber: 1g; Protein: 60g

¼ cup vegetable oil

1 medium onion, cut into slices (about 1 cup)

4 garlic cloves, minced

2 teaspoons cayenne pepper, or more to taste

2 teaspoons curry powder

1 teaspoon smoked or regular paprika

1 teaspoon kosher salt, plus more to taste

½ teaspoon ground ginger

¼ teaspoon ground cinnamon

¼ teaspoon freshly ground black pepper, plus more to taste

½ cup Chicken Stock (page 228) or low-sodium beef broth

¼ cup rice vinegar

1 (2-pound) boneless beef chuck roast, trimmed and cut into 1½-inch cubes

Steamed rice, for serving

1. Prepare the sauce. Preheat the Instant Pot® by selecting Sauté and adjust to More for high heat. (For a thicker sauce, adjust to Normal for medium heat.) Heat the oil until it shimmers. Add the onion and cook, stirring frequently, just until starting to brown, 2 to 3 minutes. Add the garlic and cook, stirring frequently, until fragrant, about 1 minute. Add the cayenne, curry powder, paprika, salt, ginger, cinnamon, and black pepper and cook, stirring constantly, until a paste forms and darkens slightly, 1 to 2 minutes. Add the stock and vinegar and bring to a simmer. Scrape any browned bits from the bottom and reduce to your preferred consistency.

2. Pressure cook. Add the beef to the Instant Pot®. Lock the lid into place. Select Manual; adjust the pressure to High and the time to 25 minutes. After cooking, naturally release the pressure for 15 minutes, then quick release any remaining pressure. Unlock and remove the lid.

3. Finish the dish. Spoon or blot off any fat on the top of the sauce. For a thicker sauce, select Sauté and adjust to Normal for medium heat. Bring the sauce to a simmer and cook until reduced to your preferred consistency. Serve with rice.

PENNE BOLOGNESE

Bolognese is a classic Italian meat sauce, fragrant with onion and deriving its flavor and body from both tomatoes and milk. Made the traditional way, it simmers for hours, but the pressure cooker version takes a fraction of the time. And as a bonus, you can cook the pasta right in the sauce, for a delicious Italian meal any night of the week. Or make the sauce without the pasta and freeze it for evenings when you need a meal that's ready to go. **SERVES 4**

PREP AND FINISHING
15 minutes

MANUAL
12 + 5 minutes
high pressure

RELEASE
Natural for
10 minutes + Quick

TOTAL TIME
50 MINUTES

60 MIN OR LESS

ONE POT

2 tablespoons extra-virgin olive oil

½ medium onion, chopped (about ½ cup)

1 garlic clove, minced

1 medium carrot, peeled and chopped (about ⅔ cup)

1 medium celery stalk, chopped (about ½ cup)

1 pound ground beef (or half ground beef and half ground pork)

1¼ teaspoons kosher salt, divided, plus more to taste

¼ cup dry white wine

1½ cups strained tomatoes or tomato sauce

½ cup milk

8 ounces penne pasta

1 cup water

2 tablespoons chopped fresh parsley

1. Start the sauce. Preheat the Instant Pot® by selecting Sauté and adjust to More for high heat. Heat the oil until it shimmers. Add the onion, garlic, carrot, and celery and cook, stirring occasionally, until the vegetables start to soften, 2 to 3 minutes. Add the ground beef and sprinkle it with ½ teaspoon of salt. Stir to break the meat into small pieces and cook just until it starts to brown, about 3 minutes. Add the wine and stir, scraping the bottom of the pot to dissolve the browned bits. Pour in the strained tomatoes, milk, and ¼ teaspoon of salt. Stir to combine.

2. Pressure cook the sauce. Lock the lid into place. Select Manual; adjust the pressure to High and the time to 12 minutes. After cooking, naturally release the pressure for 10 minutes, then quick release any remaining pressure. Unlock and remove the lid.

3. Pressure cook the pasta. Add the pasta, water, and remaining ½ teaspoon of salt. Stir to combine. Lock the lid into place. Select Manual; adjust the pressure to High and the time to 5 minutes. After cooking, quick release the pressure. Unlock and remove the lid.

4. Finish the dish. Test the pasta; it should be tender with just a slightly firm center. If not, or if the sauce is too thin, simmer everything for a few minutes. Adjust the seasoning, adding more salt if necessary. Spoon into bowls, sprinkle with the parsley, and serve.

PER SERVING Calories: 498; Fat: 16g; Sodium: 1330mg; Carbohydrates: 41g; Fiber: 2g; Protein: 44g

SPICY BROCCOLI BEEF

Broccoli cooks quickly under pressure, so it was a challenge to develop a recipe for this Chinese-American dish that could be made completely in the Instant Pot®. But since broccoli beef is one of my favorite take-out dishes, a few trial runs before I came up with the perfect version was totally worth it. Using whole sirloin steak ensures the meat doesn't overcook, and searing it provides the flavor you get from stir-frying over high heat. And since the meat cooks quickly, it can go in the pot with the broccoli and cook at the same time. **SERVES 4**

PREP AND FINISHING
20 minutes

MANUAL
1 minute
low pressure

RELEASE
Quick

**TOTAL TIME
30 MINUTES**

30 MIN OR LESS

DAIRY-FREE

2 (12- to 14-ounce) top sirloin steaks, about 1 inch thick

½ teaspoon kosher salt

3 tablespoons vegetable oil, divided

¼ cup dry sherry

12 ounces broccoli florets (about 2 medium crowns)

½ cup low-sodium beef broth

¼ cup water

¼ cup soy sauce

2 tablespoons oyster sauce

2 tablespoons rice vinegar

2 tablespoons orange juice concentrate

1 tablespoon Asian chili garlic sauce, or more to taste

2 teaspoons cornstarch

1 tablespoon minced peeled ginger

1 tablespoon minced garlic

2 scallions, sliced, white and green parts separated

Steamed rice, for serving

1. Sear the beef. Sprinkle the steaks on both sides with the salt. Heat a large cast iron or other heavy skillet on the stove over high heat. Heat 2 tablespoons of oil until it shimmers. (If you prefer to sear the steaks in the Instant Pot®, preheat the pot by selecting Sauté and adjust to More for high heat. Heat the oil until it shimmers.) Add the beef in a single layer without crowding (work in batches if necessary). Sear the beef for 1½ minutes. Flip the steaks and repeat on the other side. Transfer the beef to a rack or plate.

2. Deglaze the pan. Pour the oil out of the skillet or pot and add the sherry. Bring it to a simmer and cook, scraping the bottom of the pan to dissolve any browned bits, until the sherry has reduced by about half. Pour the reduced sherry into the Instant Pot®.

3. **Pressure cook.** Add the beef broth and water to the pot. Put the broccoli in a steamer basket or on a silicone steamer trivet and place the steaks on top of the broccoli. Place the steamer in the pot. Lock the lid into place. Select Manual; adjust the pressure to Low and the time to 1 minute. After cooking, quick release the pressure. Unlock and remove the lid. Remove the steamer basket and transfer the steaks to a plate or cutting board.

4. **Make and cook the sauce.** Pour the beef broth mixture from the pot into a small bowl. Add the soy sauce, oyster sauce, vinegar, orange juice concentrate, chili garlic sauce, and cornstarch and whisk together. Set aside. Preheat the Instant Pot® by selecting Sauté and adjust to Normal for medium heat. Heat the remaining 1 tablespoon of oil until it shimmers. Add the ginger, garlic, and the white parts of the scallions and cook, stirring frequently, until fragrant, about 2 minutes. Add the reserved beef broth mixture. Stir to combine and cook, stirring occasionally, until the sauce has thickened, 2 to 3 minutes. Adjust the heat to Less for low heat.

5. **Finish the dish.** While the sauce cooks, slice the steaks about ⅛ inch thick. If the slices are large, cut them into bite-size pieces. The steak might be raw in the center. Don't worry; it will cook again. Add the beef slices and broccoli to the sauce in the pot and stir to coat. Cook just long enough for the beef to finish cooking and the broccoli to warm through. (If the beef is quite raw in the center, add it first for a minute or so to cook further, then add the broccoli.) Serve with rice and garnish with the green parts of the scallions.

PER SERVING Calories: 532; Fat: 23g; Sodium: 1213mg; Carbohydrates: 12g; Fiber: 3g; Protein: 64g

FRUIT AND PISTACHIO CHEESECAKE (PAGE 211)

CHAPTER 9
DESSERTS

Sure, everyone knows you can cook great main dishes, with or without meat, in the Instant Pot®, not to mention side dishes or soups. But it's just as handy—and often even more impressive—for desserts. It makes the creamiest cheesecakes, puddings, and custards imaginable. You can even cook cakes, with the right recipe. Some of the recipes here are finished pretty much completely in the pot, while others use elements cooked in the pot combined with other ingredients for chilled or frozen desserts. Think outside the pot!

CARAMELIZED BANANA PUDDING

I suppose that, technically, this is more of a custard than a pudding; it's certainly not a banana pudding in the southern sense—the kind that's layered with vanilla wafer cookies and bananas. It is, however, delicious. Browning the bananas in butter and sugar gives them a deep flavor so they can stand up to the velvety creaminess of the custard. **SERVES 6**

PREP AND FINISHING
15 minutes

MANUAL
6 minutes
high pressure

RELEASE
Natural for 10 minutes

TOTAL TIME
35 MINUTES, PLUS
2 HOURS TO CHILL

GRAIN-FREE

2 tablespoons unsalted butter

2 or 3 large bananas, sliced into ¼-inch rounds

1 tablespoon brown sugar

6 large egg yolks

1 teaspoon vanilla extract

⅔ cup granulated sugar

1 cup whole milk

1 cup heavy (whipping) cream

1 cup water, for steaming

1. **Prepare the bananas.** Melt the butter in a medium skillet over medium heat. When it has stopped foaming and is just starting to brown, add the banana slices in a single layer. Cook for 1 minute, then turn them over and cook for 1 minute more. Push the bananas to the sides of the skillet and add the brown sugar. Let it cook, stirring, for 2 minutes, until melted and bubbling. Move the banana slices into the sugar and stir to coat. Remove the skillet from the heat and set aside.

2. **Make the custard.** In a medium bowl, beat the egg yolks, vanilla, and granulated sugar with a hand mixer until the sugar is dissolved. Add the milk and cream and beat briefly to combine.

3. **Prepare the ramekins.** Divide the bananas among 6 small (1- to 1½-cup) ramekins or custard cups. Gently pour the custard over the bananas.

4. Pressure cook. Pour the water into the Instant Pot®. Place a trivet in the pot and place the ramekins on top, stacking them if necessary. Drape a piece of aluminum foil over the ramekins to keep condensation off the top of the puddings. Lock the lid into place. Select Manual; adjust the pressure to High and the time to 6 minutes. After cooking, naturally release the pressure for 10 minutes, then quick release any remaining pressure. Unlock and remove the lid.

5. Chill the pudding. Carefully remove the foil and use tongs to remove the puddings from the pot. Let cool at room temperature for 20 minutes or so, then refrigerate until chilled, 1 to 2 hours, before serving.

PER SERVING Calories: 324; Fat: 17g; Sodium: 60mg; Carbohydrates: 40g; Fiber: 2g; Protein: 5g

CRÈME BRÛLÉE

The first time I had crème brûlée was on a field trip with my junior high school French class to a local French restaurant. I was initially hesitant, since I wasn't a fan of custard, but I was won over by the cool, rich, creamy base topped with crisp, caramelized sugar. I've tried to recapture that experience with this recipe. If you prefer a warm custard, you can finish the desserts without refrigerating. **SERVES 6**

PREP AND FINISHING
15 minutes

MANUAL
6 minutes
high pressure

RELEASE
Natural for 10 minutes

**TOTAL TIME
35 MINUTES, PLUS
2 HOURS TO CHILL**

GRAIN-FREE

8 large egg yolks

1 teaspoon vanilla extract

½ cup granulated sugar

2 cups heavy (whipping) cream

1 cup water, for steaming

6 tablespoons light brown sugar, sifted

1. Make the custard. In a medium bowl, beat the egg yolks, vanilla, and granulated sugar with a hand mixer until the sugar is dissolved. Add the cream and beat briefly to combine. Pour into 6 small (1- to 1½-cup) ramekins or custard cups. You may find it easier to do this if you transfer the custard to a measuring cup with a lip, making it easier and less messy to pour.

2. Pressure cook. Pour the water into the Instant Pot®. Place a trivet in the pot and place the ramekins on top, stacking them if necessary. Drape a piece of aluminum foil over the ramekins to keep condensation off the top of the puddings. Lock the lid into place. Select Manual; adjust the pressure to High and the time to 6 minutes. After cooking, naturally release the pressure for 10 minutes, then quick release any remaining pressure. Unlock and remove the lid. Carefully remove the foil and use tongs to remove the ramekins from the pot. Let cool at room temperature for 20 minutes or so, then refrigerate until chilled, about 2 hours.

3. Finish the crème brûlée. Sprinkle the brown sugar evenly over the tops of the puddings. Use a kitchen torch to brown the sugar, or place the ramekins on a baking sheet and place under a very hot broiler until the tops are browned, 1 to 2 minutes. Watch them carefully, as they can go from browned to burned very quickly. Serve.

PER SERVING Calories: 309; Fat: 21g; Sodium: 29mg; Carbohydrates: 28g; Fiber: 0g; Protein: 4g

CHEESECAKE
FOUR WAYS

Right after eggs, beans, and rice, the dish most cooks are excited to cook in the Instant Pot® is cheesecake. It's easy to see why: The steamy environment of a pressure cooker results in amazingly smooth and creamy cheesecake, and it's not that difficult to make. Once you get the basic recipe down, experiment with these great variations, or develop your own! **SERVES 8**

PREP
25 minutes

MANUAL
25 minutes
high pressure

RELEASE
Natural for 10 minutes

**TOTAL TIME
1 HOUR 10 MINUTES,
PLUS 4 HOURS
TO CHILL**

CORE INGREDIENTS

4 ounces graham crackers, crushed into crumbs (about 1 cup crumbs)

2 tablespoons unsalted butter, melted

16 ounces cream cheese, at room temperature

½ cup sugar

2 large eggs

1 cup water, for steaming

FOR NEW YORK CHEESECAKE

⅔ cup plus 2 tablespoons sour cream, divided

2 tablespoons heavy (whipping) cream

1 teaspoon vanilla extract

1 teaspoon grated lemon zest

1 tablespoon sugar

FOR FRUIT AND PISTACHIO CHEESECAKE

2 tablespoons sour cream

2 tablespoons heavy (whipping) cream

1 teaspoon vanilla extract

1 teaspoon grated lemon zest

½ cup toasted pistachios, divided

1 cup frozen raspberries, thawed

2 tablespoons raspberry liqueur

2 tablespoons granulated sugar

½ cup fresh raspberries

1 plum, sliced thin (optional)

FOR LEMON-BLUEBERRY CHEESECAKE

2 tablespoons sour cream

2 tablespoons heavy (whipping) cream

1 teaspoon vanilla extract

2 teaspoons lemon zest

½ cup blueberries

1 cup Lemon Curd (page 234)

FOR IRISH CREAM CHEESECAKE

¼ cup Irish cream liqueur

1 teaspoon vanilla extract

1 teaspoon grated lemon zest

1 cup Chocolate-Caramel Sauce (page 241) ➤

1. **Make the crust.** Preheat the oven to 350°F. In a small bowl, mix the graham cracker crumbs with the melted butter. Press the crumbs into the bottom of a 7-inch springform pan and up the sides about ½ inch. Bake until fragrant and set, 5 to 6 minutes. Let cool.

2. **Make the filling.** Beat the cream cheese in a medium bowl with a hand mixer until very smooth. Add the sugar and beat until well blended.

For New York Cheesecake: Add 2 tablespoons of sour cream, the heavy cream, the vanilla, and the lemon zest and beat to combine.

For Fruit and Pistachio Cheesecake: Add the sour cream, heavy cream, vanilla, and lemon zest and beat to combine.

For Lemon-Blueberry Cheesecake: Add the sour cream, heavy cream, vanilla, and lemon zest and beat to combine.

For Irish Cream Cheesecake: Add the Irish cream, vanilla, and lemon zest and beat to combine.

For all variations: Add the eggs, one at a time, and beat until incorporated.

For Fruit and Pistachio Cheesecake: Finely chop ¼ cup of the pistachios and gently fold them into the batter.

3. **Assemble the cheesecake.**

For Lemon-Blueberry Cheesecake: Pour half of the batter into the prepared crust and distribute the blueberries evenly over the top, then pour the remaining batter over the blueberries.

For the other variations: Pour the cheesecake mixture into the prepared crust.

For all variations: Gently smooth the top. Place a piece of aluminum foil over the top, and be sure to crimp it over the sides of the pan.

4. Pressure cook. Pour the water into the Instant Pot®. Place a trivet with handles in the pot and place the pan on top. If your trivet doesn't have handles, use a foil sling (see page 16) to make removing the pan easier. Lock the lid into place. Select Manual; adjust the pressure to High and the time to 25 minutes. After cooking, naturally release the pressure for 10 minutes, then quick release any remaining pressure. Carefully remove the cheesecake from the pot and remove the foil. The cheesecake should be set, with the center slightly softer than the edges.

5. Chill the cheesecake.

For New York Cheesecake: Mix the remaining ⅔ cup of sour cream and the sugar in a small bowl. Spread this mixture over the hot cheesecake.

For all variations: Let the cheesecake rest at room temperature for 15 to 20 minutes, then refrigerate until thoroughly chilled, 3 to 4 hours.

6. Finish the cheesecake. Remove the sides of the springform pan.

For New York Cheesecake: Serve.

For Fruit and Pistachio Cheesecake: In a blender or small food processor, purée the frozen raspberries, raspberry liqueur, and sugar. Strain into a small bowl or squeeze bottle. Drizzle over the top of the cheesecake. Top with the fresh raspberries, remaining ¼ cup of pistachios, and plum (if using) and serve.

For Lemon-Blueberry Cheesecake: Spread the lemon curd over the top of the cheesecake and serve.

For Irish Cream Cheesecake: Spread the chocolate-caramel sauce over the top of the cheesecake and serve.

MARBLED-CREAM CHEESE PUMPKIN PIE

While some people, like my sister, are huge fans of pumpkin pie, it's never been one of my favorites. This delicious version satisfies both of us. It contains enough pumpkin and spices to please a Thanksgiving traditionalist, but the addition of cream cheese and sour cream lightens the texture, giving me a pumpkin pie I look forward to any time of year. **SERVES 6**

PREP
25 minutes

MANUAL
30 minutes
high pressure

RELEASE
Natural for 10 minutes

TOTAL TIME
1 HOUR
10 MINUTES, PLUS
4 HOURS TO CHILL

4 ounces gingersnap cookies (about 10)

⅓ cup finely chopped pecans

2 tablespoons unsalted butter, melted

8 ounces cream cheese, at room temperature

6 tablespoons sour cream, at room temperature

½ cup sugar

2 large eggs

1 cup canned pumpkin purée (not pumpkin pie filling)

½ teaspoon ground cinnamon

¼ teaspoon ground ginger

⅛ teaspoon ground cloves

⅛ teaspoon ground allspice

⅛ teaspoon ground nutmeg

1 cup water, for steaming

Whipped cream, for garnish

1. Make the crust. Preheat the oven to 350°F. Crush the cookies into fine crumbs in a small food processor or in a zip-top bag using a rolling pin. You should have about 1 cup of crumbs. Transfer to a small bowl and stir in the pecans and melted butter. Press the crumbs into the bottom of a 7-inch springform pan and up the sides about ½ inch. Bake until fragrant and set, 5 to 6 minutes. Let cool.

2. Make the filling. In a medium bowl, beat the cream cheese and sour cream with a hand mixer until very smooth. Add about half of the sugar and beat until well blended. Add the remaining sugar and beat again. Add the eggs and beat until they are just incorporated. Remove about ¼ cup of this cream cheese mixture and set aside. Add the pumpkin purée, cinnamon, ginger, cloves, allspice, and nutmeg to the cream cheese mixture in the bowl and beat until well blended.

3. Assemble the pie. Pour the pumpkin mixture into the pre-pared crust. Depending on the depth of your pan, you may not need quite all of it. It should come up to about an inch from the top of the pan. Drop spoonfuls of the reserved cream cheese mixture evenly on top of the pumpkin filling. Run the tip of a small knife or a skewer through the filling to form a swirled ("marbleized") pattern on the top of the pie.

4. Pressure cook the pie. Pour the water into the Instant Pot®. Place a trivet with handles in the pot and place the pan on top. If your trivet doesn't have handles, use a foil sling (see page 16) to make removing the pan easier. Lay a piece of aluminum foil over the top of the bowl to prevent condensation from forming on top of the pie. Lock the lid into place. Select Manual; adjust the pressure to High and the time to 30 minutes. After cooking, naturally release the pressure for 10 minutes, then quick release any remaining pressure. Unlock and remove the lid. Carefully remove the pie from the pot and remove the foil. The pie should be set fully.

5. Chill and finish the pie. Let the pie rest at room temperature for 10 to 20 minutes, then refrigerate until chilled, 3 to 4 hours. Remove the sides of the pan, garnish with the whipped cream, and serve.

INGREDIENT TIP: Don't have all those spices on hand? Don't worry! You can use 1 teaspoon of pumpkin pie spice instead.

PER SERVING Calories: 327; Fat: 25g; Sodium: 171mg; Carbohydrates: 23g; Fiber: 2g; Protein: 6g

CHOCOLATE PUDDING

Chocolate pudding is one of those childhood comfort foods that remain just as good when you grow up. This version is silky and doubly chocolaty, with cocoa powder and melted bittersweet chocolate. (There's no such thing as too much chocolate, right?) This recipe makes a fairly soft pudding; if you prefer a firmer pudding, add the optional cornstarch. **SERVES 6**

PREP AND FINISHING
15 minutes

MANUAL
9 minutes
high pressure

RELEASE
Natural for 10 minutes

TOTAL TIME
40 MINUTES, PLUS
2 HOURS TO CHILL

GRAIN-FREE

2 large eggs

⅓ cup sugar

2 cups whole milk

⅓ cup unsweetened cocoa powder

2 teaspoons vanilla extract, divided

1 tablespoon cornstarch (optional)

Pinch salt

1 cup water, for steaming

3 ounces bittersweet chocolate, chopped

¼ cup heavy (whipping) cream

Whipped cream, for serving (optional)

1. Mix the ingredients. In a heat-proof bowl that will fit in the Instant Pot®, beat the eggs and sugar with a hand mixer until the sugar has mostly dissolved. Add half of the milk and half of the cocoa powder and beat to combine. Add the rest of the milk and cocoa powder, along with 1 teaspoon of vanilla, the cornstarch (if using), and the salt. The mixture will probably appear grainy, but that's okay. Cover the bowl with aluminum foil.

2. Pressure cook the pudding. Pour the water into the Instant Pot®. Place a trivet with handles in the pot and place the bowl on top. If your trivet doesn't have handles, use a foil sling (see page 16) to make removing the bowl easier. Lock the lid into place. Select Manual; adjust the pressure to High and the time to 9 minutes. After cooking, naturally release the pressure for 10 minutes, then quick release any remaining pressure. Unlock and remove the lid. Carefully remove the bowl from the Instant Pot and remove the foil. The mixture will appear clumpy and curdled. ➤

3. **Mix the cholocate and cream.** While the pudding is cooking, combine the chocolate and cream in a small microwave-safe bowl and microwave for 25 seconds. Take the bowl out and stir the mixture. Repeat until the chocolate is mostly melted, another 10 to 15 seconds.

4. **Finish the pudding.** With the hand mixer, blend the pudding until it begins to smooth out. Add the cream and chocolate and the remaining 1 teaspoon of vanilla and continue to beat until completely smooth. Spoon the pudding into 6 small (1- to 1½-cup) ramekins or custard cups. Refrigerate until set, 2 to 4 hours. Serve topped with whipped cream (if using).

PER SERVING Calories: 333; Fat: 17g; Sodium: 144mg; Carbohydrates: 39g; Fiber: 3g; Protein: 10g

LEMON-GINGERSNAP PARFAITS

My dad loved his desserts. He was happy enough with ice cream most nights, but once in a while, my mom would indulge him and make parfaits with crushed gingersnaps, applesauce, and whipped cream. It was one of our favorite desserts—she used commercial cookies and applesauce, but even so, the parfaits were more than the sum of their parts. These days, I've appropriated her idea, but I substitute lemon curd for the applesauce for a richer, tangier version. **SERVES 6**

PREP
25 minutes

**TOTAL TIME
25 MINUTES,
PLUS 20 MINUTES
TO CHILL**

60 MIN OR LESS

16 ounces gingersnap cookies

1 cup heavy (whipping) cream

1 teaspoon confectioners' sugar

1 recipe Lemon Curd (page 234)

1. Prep the ingredients. Crush the cookies into fine crumbs in a food processor or in a zip-top bag using a rolling pin (you should have 2 to 3 cups). In a medium bowl, whip the cream with a hand mixer until it is frothy. Add the confectioners' sugar and continue whipping until soft peaks form.

2. Make the parfaits. Spoon a ¼-inch-thick layer of cookie crumbs into the bottom of each of 6 small wine glasses. Cover each crumb layer with 1 tablespoon of the whipped cream. Top with a ¼-inch-thick layer of lemon curd. Add a ¼-inch-thick layer of whipped cream. Add a ¼-inch-thick layer of crumbs. Repeat the ingredients until the glasses are full or you run out of ingredients. Top with a final sprinkling of cookie crumbs. Chill for 20 minutes to set and hydrate the cookie crumbs.

PER SERVING Calories: 464; Fat: 22g; Sodium: 326mg; Carbohydrates: 56g; Fiber: 1g; Protein: 5g

BROWNED-BUTTER APPLE SPICE CAKE

Many years ago, I discovered the combination of browned butter, cinnamon, and cardamom in desserts. I've used it in cookies and pies, but it truly shines in cakes, especially if apples are involved. This recipe produces a slightly dense, very moist cake. It makes a wonderful dessert, but since it contains fruit and yogurt, you might want to enjoy it for breakfast. I won't tell. **SERVES 6**

PREP AND FINISHING
25 minutes

MANUAL
18 minutes
high pressure

RELEASE
Natural for 10 minutes

**TOTAL TIME
1 HOUR**

60 MIN OR LESS

6 tablespoons unsalted butter, plus additional to grease the pan

1 large egg

1 cup Greek-Style Yogurt (page 230)

⅓ cup granulated sugar

1 teaspoon vanilla extract

1 cup all-purpose flour

2 teaspoons baking powder

¼ teaspoon ground cinnamon

⅛ teaspoon ground cardamom

1 medium apple, peeled, cored, and diced

1 cup water, for steaming

¼ cup confectioners' sugar

1. Brown the butter. In a small saucepan over medium heat, cook the butter until the milk solids begin to brown, 3 to 5 minutes. Measure out 3 tablespoons of butter into a medium bowl and set the rest of the butter in the pan aside.

2. Prepare the pan. Lightly grease a 6- or 7-inch springform pan (or cake pan with a removable bottom) with butter.

3. Make the batter. In the bowl with the 3 tablespoons of browned butter, stir in the egg, yogurt, granulated sugar, and vanilla. In a small bowl, sift together the flour, baking powder, cinnamon, and cardamom. Add these dry ingredients to the wet ingredients. Stir until just combined. Stir in the apple. Pour the batter into the prepared pan.

4. **Pressure cook the cake.** Pour the water into the Instant Pot®. Place a trivet with handles in the pot and place the pan on top. If your trivet doesn't have handles, use a foil sling (see page 16) to make removing the pan easier. Lock the lid into place. Select Manual; adjust the pressure to High and the time to 18 minutes. After cooking, naturally release the pressure for 10 minutes, then manually release any remaining pressure. Unlock and remove the lid.

5. **Finish the cake.** Remove the pan from the pot. Let the cake cool for 5 to 10 minutes, then remove the sides of the pan. Let the cake cool for another 10 minutes. Reheat the remaining browned butter if it's solidified, and drizzle it over the cake. Dust with the confectioners' sugar and serve.

PER SERVING Calories: 303; Fat: 13g; Sodium: 124mg; Carbohydrates: 41g; Fiber: 2g; Protein: 6g

FROZEN CREAMSICLE PIE

Frozen pie from a pressure cooker? Not really, but you can make the curd for the filling, which is the only fussy thing about this recipe. I love the combination of orange and vanilla—when I was a kid, Creamsicles were always my favorite ice cream bar. This is like a grown-up version of that treat, but even better since it's made with real orange juice and cream. **SERVES 8**

PREP AND FINISHING
25 minutes

MANUAL
10 minutes
high pressure

RELEASE
Natural for 10 minutes

**TOTAL TIME
1 HOUR, PLUS
8 HOURS TO CHILL**

6 ounces vanilla wafer cookies

7 tablespoons unsalted butter, 3 melted and 4 at room temperature, divided

1 cup freshly squeezed orange juice

½ cup sugar

4 large egg yolks

2 teaspoons grated orange zest

Pinch salt

1 cup water, for steaming

½ cup heavy (whipping) cream, very cold

1 teaspoon orange juice concentrate

½ teaspoon vanilla extract

FOR THE TOPPING

½ cup heavy (whipping) cream, cold

1 teaspoon orange juice concentrate

½ teaspoon vanilla extract

1. **Make the crust.** Preheat the oven to 350°F. Crush the cookies into fine crumbs in a small food processor or in a zip-top bag using a rolling pin. Transfer to a small bowl and stir in the 3 tablespoons of melted butter. Press the crumbs into the bottom and up the sides of a 9-inch pie plate. Bake until fragrant and set, 6 to 8 minutes. Let cool. (The cooled crust can be stored in the freezer until the filling is ready. Alternatively, you can make the crust while the curd chills; just be sure it's completely cool before the filling goes in.)

2. **Reduce the orange juice.** In a small saucepan, simmer the orange juice over medium heat until reduced to ⅓ cup.

3. **Mix the filling ingredients.** In a heat-proof bowl that will fit in the Instant Pot®, beat the sugar and the 4 tablespoons of room-temperature butter with a hand mixer until the sugar has mostly dissolved and the mixture is light colored and fluffy. Add the egg yolks and beat until just combined. Add the reduced

orange juice, the orange zest, and salt and beat to combine. The mixture will probably appear grainy, but that's okay. Cover the bowl with aluminum foil.

4. Pressure cook the curd. Pour the water into the Instant Pot®. Place a trivet with handles in the pot and place the bowl on top. If your trivet doesn't have handles, use a foil sling (see page 16) to make removing the bowl easier. Lock the lid into place. Select Manual; adjust the pressure to High and the time to 10 minutes. After cooking, naturally release the pressure for 10 minutes, then quick release any remaining pressure. Unlock and remove the lid. Carefully remove the bowl from the pot and remove the foil. The mixture will appear clumpy and curdled.

5. Finish the curd. Whisk the curd mixture until smooth. Place a fine-mesh strainer over a medium bowl and pour the curd through it, pressing down with a flexible spatula to pass the curd through, leaving the zest and any curdled egg bits behind. Be sure to scrape any curd on the outside bottom of the strainer into the bowl. Cover the bowl with plastic wrap, pushing the wrap down on top of the curd to keep a skin from forming. Refrigerate until set, 2 to 4 hours.

6. Make the pie filling. Pour the very cold cream into a medium bowl and add the orange juice concentrate and vanilla. Using a hand mixer, whip the cream until soft peaks form. Spoon about two-thirds of the whipped cream onto the chilled curd in the bowl. Beat on medium-high speed until thoroughly combined. Gently fold in the remaining whipped cream by hand. Pour the orange cream into the crumb crust and place in the freezer until frozen, 4 to 6 hours.

7. Make the topping. Beat the cold cream, orange juice concentrate, and vanilla to moderately stiff peaks. Spoon over the pie just before serving.

PER SERVING Calories: 325; Fat: 21g; Sodium: 167mg; Carbohydrates: 32g; Fiber: 1g; Protein: 3g

MARGARITA PIE

Like the Frozen Creamsicle Pie (page 222), this recipe combines a tart citrus curd with whipped cream for a silky frozen pie. This one is flavored with just a hint of tequila and orange, for a dessert reminiscent of the best margarita in town! **SERVES 8**

(page 222)

PREP AND FINISHING
25 minutes

MANUAL
10 minutes
high pressure

RELEASE
Natural for 10 minutes

TOTAL TIME
50 MINUTES, PLUS
8 HOURS TO CHILL

6 ounces salted pretzels

7 tablespoons unsalted butter, 3 melted and 4 at room temperature, divided

¾ cup sugar

4 large egg yolks

2 teaspoons grated lime zest

6 tablespoons freshly squeezed lime juice

1 teaspoon orange juice concentrate

Pinch salt

1 cup water, for steaming

½ cup heavy (whipping) cream, very cold

2 tablespoons tequila

FOR THE TOPPING

½ cup heavy (whipping) cream, cold

1 tablespoon tequila

1 teaspoon orange juice concentrate

1. Make the crust. Preheat the oven to 350°F. Crush the pretzels into fine crumbs in a small food processor or in a zip-top bag using a rolling pin. Transfer the crumbs to a small bowl and stir in the 3 tablespoons of melted butter. Press the crumbs into the bottom and up the sides of a 9-inch pie plate. Bake until fragrant, 6 to 8 minutes. Let cool. (The cooled crust can be stored in the freezer until the filling is ready. Alternatively, you can make the crust while the curd chills; just be sure it's completely cool before the filling goes in.)

2. Mix the filling ingredients. In a heat-proof bowl that will fit in the Instant Pot®, beat the sugar and the 4 tablespoons of room-temperature butter with a hand mixer until the sugar has mostly dissolved and the mixture is light colored and fluffy. Add the egg yolks and beat until combined. Add the lime zest and juice, orange juice concentrate, and salt and beat to combine. The mixture will probably appear grainy, but that's okay. Cover the bowl with aluminum foil.

3. Pressure cook the curd. Pour the water into the Instant Pot®. Place a trivet with handles in the pot and place the bowl on top. If your trivet doesn't have handles, use a foil sling (see page 16) to make removing the bowl easier. Lock the lid into place. Select Manual; adjust the pressure to High and the time to 10 minutes. After cooking, naturally release the pressure for 10 minutes, then quick release any remaining pressure. Unlock and remove the lid. Carefully remove the bowl from the pot and remove the foil. The mixture will appear clumpy and curdled.

4. Finish the curd. Whisk the curd mixture until smooth. Place a fine-mesh strainer over a medium bowl and pour the curd through it, pressing down with a flexible spatula to pass the curd through, leaving the zest and any curdled egg bits behind. Be sure to scrape any curd on the outside bottom of the strainer into the bowl. Cover the bowl with plastic wrap, pushing the wrap down on top of the curd to keep a skin from forming. Refrigerate until set, 2 to 4 hours.

5. Make the pie filling. Pour the very cold cream into a medium bowl and add the tequila. Using a hand mixer, whip the cream and tequila until soft peaks form. Spoon about two-thirds of the whipped cream onto the chilled curd in the bowl. Beat on medium-high speed until thoroughly combined. Gently fold in the remaining whipped cream by hand. Pour the lime cream into the crumb crust and place in the freezer until frozen, 4 to 6 hours.

6. Make the topping. Beat the cold cream, tequila, and orange juice concentrate to moderately stiff peaks. Spoon over the pie just before serving.

INGREDIENT TIP: Although there is not much tequila in this dessert, it is not cooked at all, so if you are serving children or guests with alcohol sensitivity, you can just leave it out.

PER SERVING Calories: 335; Fat: 19g; Sodium: 392mg; Carbohydrates: 37g; Fiber: 1g; Protein: 4g

CHICKEN STOCK (PAGE 228)

CHAPTER 10
KITCHEN STAPLES

Whether they're for stocks or sauces or yogurt, the recipes in this chapter will give you the building blocks to make amazing soups, entrées, breakfasts, and desserts. While there are commercial versions of almost all these products, making your own gives you complete control over what goes into them. Bonus: It's really fun! Most can be frozen, so you can spend a weekend cooking and stock up on these basics for months. And some, like Lemon Curd and Chocolate-Caramel Sauce, make wonderful gifts for friends and family.

CHICKEN STOCK

If you haven't used your Instant Pot® to make stock, you don't know what you're missing. Ninety minutes and very little work yield a savory stock that tastes like it had simmered for hours. Many recipes for chicken stock call for the addition of vegetables and herbs, but I've come to prefer it without these, as they can become bitter if overcooked and tend to mask the chicken flavor. **MAKES 1 QUART**

PREP AND FINISHING
20 minutes

MANUAL
90 minutes
high pressure

RELEASE
Natural for 15 minutes

**TOTAL TIME
2 HOURS
10 MINUTES,
PLUS OVERNIGHT
TO CHILL**

GRAIN-FREE

DAIRY-FREE

2 pounds meaty chicken bones (backs, wing tips, leg quarters)

¼ teaspoon kosher salt

1 quart water, or more if needed

½ teaspoon kosher salt (optional)

1. Pressure cook. Pile the chicken bones in the Instant Pot® and sprinkle with the ¼ teaspoon salt. Add the water, adding more if necessary just to cover the bones but not filling the pot more than half full with water. Select Manual; adjust the pressure to High and the time to 90 minutes. After cooking, naturally release for 15 minutes, then quick release any remaining pressure. Unlock and remove the lid.

2. Strain the stock. Line a colander with cheesecloth or a clean cotton towel (you'll never get the towel completely clean, so don't use a nice one) and place it over a large bowl. Pour the chicken parts and stock into the colander to strain out the meat and bones. Discard the solids. Let the stock cool and then refrigerate for several hours or overnight so that the fat hardens on the top of the stock.

3. Finish the stock. Peel the layer of fat off the stock. Measure the amount of stock. If you have more than 1 quart (you probably will), pour the stock into a pot and bring it to a boil on the stove. Reduce the stock until you have a quart. If you like, add the ½ teaspoon salt to approximate the salt level of commercial low-sodium stocks. The stock can be refrigerated for several days or frozen for several months in airtight containers.

PER SERVING (1 CUP) Calories: 66; Fat: 2g; Sodium: 67mg; Carbohydrates: 5g; Fiber: 0g; Protein: 6g

VEGETABLE STOCK

Vegetable stock is fast and easy to make, so there's really no excuse not to keep it on hand for all kinds of recipes. Browning the onions before pressure cooking develops a deeper flavor, and the mushrooms contribute a savory "umami" quality that will enliven any dish where the stock is used. **MAKES 1 QUART**

PREP AND FINISHING
20 minutes

MANUAL
60 minutes
high pressure

RELEASE
Natural for 15 minutes

**TOTAL TIME
1 HOUR
40 MINUTES**

GRAIN-FREE

DAIRY-FREE

1 tablespoon vegetable oil

1 onion, sliced

12 ounces mushrooms, washed and sliced

2 large carrots, peeled and cut into 1-inch pieces

¼ teaspoon kosher salt

1 quart water

½ teaspoon kosher salt (optional)

1. Brown the onion. Preheat the Instant Pot® by selecting Sauté and adjust to More for high heat. Heat the oil until it shimmers. Add the onion and stir to coat with the oil. Cook the onion, stirring occasionally, until quite browned but not charred, 4 to 5 minutes.

2. Pressure cook. Add the mushrooms and carrots to the Instant Pot® and sprinkle with the ¼ teaspoon salt. Add the water. Select Manual; adjust the pressure to High and the time to 60 minutes. After cooking, naturally release the pressure for 15 minutes, then quick release any remaining pressure. Unlock and remove the lid.

3. Strain the stock. Line a colander with cheesecloth or a clean cotton towel (you'll never get the towel completely clean, so don't use a nice one) and place it over a large bowl. Pour the vegetables and stock into the colander. Discard the solids.

4. Finish the stock. Measure the amount of stock. If you have more than 1 quart, pour the stock into a pot and bring it to a boil. Reduce the stock until you have a quart. If you like, add the salt to approximate the salt level of commercial low-sodium stocks. The stock can be refrigerated for several days or frozen for several months in airtight containers.

PER SERVING (1 CUP) Calories: 34; Fat: 3g; Sodium: 148mg; Carbohydrates: 3g; Fiber: 1g; Protein: 0g

YOGURT OR GREEK-STYLE YOGURT
FOUR WAYS

There are many ways to make yogurt, with or without an Instant Pot®. But if you're looking for a simple, almost completely hands-off method, you'll agree this recipe is the way to go, whether you prefer regular or Greek-style yogurt. I don't flavor the whole batch of yogurt, because I cook with plain yogurt a lot—for instance, I use it for Better Than Mom's Potato Salad (page 72) and remoulade sauce for my Peel-and-Eat Shrimp (page 122), and I also use it for baking. I do like it flavored for breakfast, so I just flavor it right before eating. That way, I can have a variety of flavor combinations. **MAKES 8 (8-OUNCE) SERVINGS**

PREP
15 minutes

YOGURT SETTING
About 25 minutes
+ 8 to 10 hours

**TOTAL TIME
9 TO 11 HOURS,
PLUS TIME TO COOL**

GRAIN-FREE

CORE INGREDIENTS

2 quarts whole milk

1 tablespoon plain whole milk yogurt with live cultures, at room temperature

FOR LEMON YOGURT (PER 1 CUP YOGURT)

2 tablespoons Lemon Curd (page 234)

FOR STRAWBERRY YOGURT "ROMANOFF" (PER 1 CUP YOGURT)

¼ cup sliced fresh or frozen strawberries, thawed

1 tablespoon brown sugar

FOR RASPBERRY-PEACH YOGURT (PER 1 CUP YOGURT)

1 tablespoon seedless raspberry jam

¼ cup chopped fresh or frozen (thawed) peaches

FOR VANILLA-ALMOND YOGURT (PER 1 CUP YOGURT)

¼ teaspoon vanilla extract

2 drops almond extract

1 tablespoon honey

1 tablespoon toasted slivered almonds

1. Heat the milk. Pour the milk into the Instant Pot®. Select Yogurt and press Adjust so that BOIL shows in the display. Lock the lid into place. When the beeper sounds, unlock and remove the lid. Use a meat or candy thermometer to check the temperature of the milk in the center of the pot. It should read between 179°F and 182°F.

2. Cool the milk. Fill a large bowl with ice water and nestle the inner pot in it to cool the milk. If you don't have a large enough bowl to fit the pot, fill your sink with ice water to a depth of several inches and place the pot in the sink. Stir the milk occasionally, without scraping the bottom of the pot, for about 5 minutes, then take the temperature in the center of the milk. It should read between 110°F and 115°F. Remove the pot from the ice bath and dry off the outside of the pot.

3. Add the culture. In a small bowl, stir together the yogurt and about ½ cup of the warm milk. Add this to the pot and stir thoroughly but gently. Again, don't scrape the bottom of the pot (if there is any coagulated milk on the bottom, stirring it in can make your yogurt less smooth).

4. Finish the yogurt. Lock the lid into place (or use a glass lid) and select Yogurt. The display should read 8:00, which indicates 8 hours of incubation time. If you prefer a longer incubation, press the + button to increase the time by increments of 30 minutes. I prefer 10 hours for a tangy yogurt. When the yogurt cycle is complete, unlock and remove the lid. Remove the inner pot and cover it with a glass or silicone lid, or place a plate on top. Refrigerate until cool, about 4 hours, before using or stirring.

For Greek-style yogurt: After removing the inner pot from the Instant Pot®, you'll want to drain the yogurt. Line a colander or very large sieve with cheesecloth. Place the colander over a large bowl. Spoon the yogurt into the colander and let it drain for 15 to 30 minutes, depending on how thick you want your yogurt. ➤

5. **For flavored yogurt.** Measure out 1 cup of yogurt into a bowl.

For Lemon Yogurt: Stir in the lemon curd.

For Strawberry Yogurt "Romanoff": Toss the strawberries with the brown sugar to coat them. Gently fold the strawberries into the yogurt.

For Raspberry-Peach Yogurt: Fold the raspberry jam and peaches into the yogurt.

For Vanilla-Almond Yogurt: Stir in the vanilla, almond extract, and honey. Top with the toasted almonds.

COOKING TIP: I like my yogurt on the tart side. If you like yours milder, there are several things you can do. First, let it incubate for only 8 hours instead of 10. Second, drain it—much of the acidity is in the whey (the watery part). Third, increase the sweeteners when you're flavoring it.

PER SERVING Calories: 148; Fat: 8g; Sodium: 99mg; Carbohydrates: 11g; Fiber: 0g; Protein: 8g

PER SERVING (LEMON YOGURT VARIATION) Calories: 157; Fat: 9g; Sodium: 105mg; Carbohydrates: 12g; Fiber: 0g; Protein: 9g

PER SERVING (STRAWBERRY YOGURT "ROMANOFF" VARIATION) Calories: 154; Fat: 8g; Sodium: 99mg; Carbohydrates: 13g; Fiber: 0g; Protein: 8g

PER SERVING (RASPBERRY-PEACH YOGURT VARIATION) Calories: 157; Fat: 8g; Sodium: 100mg; Carbohydrates: 13g; Fiber: 0g; Protein: 8g

PER SERVING (VANILLA-ALMOND YOGURT VARIATION) Calories: 160; Fat: 8g; Sodium: 99mg; Carbohydrates: 14g; Fiber: 0g; Protein: 8g

GARLIC-HERB CHEESE SPREAD

I came up with this yogurt cheese spread when I needed an appetizer for a Middle Eastern–themed menu. I scooped out the center of thick slices of cucumber and piped the cheese in—it was a huge hit. I now use the spread for all kinds of appetizer platters, with either crackers or vegetables. It also makes a wonderful sandwich spread. **MAKES 1 CUP**

PREP
25 minutes

**TOTAL TIME
25 MINUTES,
PLUS 8 HOURS
TO DRAIN AND
1 HOUR TO CHILL**

GRAIN-FREE

2 cups plain Yogurt (page 230)

1 tablespoon extra-virgin olive oil

1 teaspoon minced garlic

1 tablespoon minced fresh parsley

2 teaspoons minced fresh chives

1 teaspoon minced fresh dill

1 teaspoon kosher salt, or to taste

1. Drain the yogurt. Line a large colander with cheesecloth or a large basket-style coffee filter and place the colander over a large bowl. Spoon in the yogurt and cover it with the edges of the cheesecloth. Place a plate over the covered yogurt and weight it down with a small can or a small bowl filled with water. Refrigerate and let drain for at least 8 hours or overnight. Pour off the liquid from time to time if the bottom of the strainer is sitting in the liquid.

2. Finish the cheese spread. When the yogurt has drained, it should be the consistency of room-temperature cream cheese; if not, drain it for another couple of hours. Stir in the olive oil, garlic, parsley, chives, dill, and salt. Return to the refrigerator for an hour or so (or up to overnight) to let the flavors mellow and meld before serving.

PER SERVING (2 TABLESPOONS) Calories: 60; Fat: 3g; Sodium: 334mg; Carbohydrates: 5g; Fiber: 0g; Protein: 4g

LEMON CURD

I love lemon curd. Silky-smooth and tangy, it's delicious over scones for break-fast, mixed into yogurt, or baked onto shortbread for the best lemon bars ever. I've been making it for almost as long as I've been cooking, and I long ago per-fected my recipe and technique. Until, that is, I read about making it in a pressure cooker. No more standing over the stove, whisking constantly to make sure it doesn't curdle. I didn't think it was possible, but lemon curd just got even better.

MAKES 1½ CUPS

PREP AND FINISHING
15 minutes

MANUAL
10 minutes
high pressure

RELEASE
10 minutes natural

**TOTAL TIME
40 MINUTES, PLUS
2 HOURS TO CHILL**

GRAIN-FREE

¾ cup sugar

4 tablespoons unsalted butter, at room temperature

4 large egg yolks

Grated zest and juice of 2 lemons (about 6 tablespoons juice)

Pinch salt

1 cup water, for steaming

1. Mix the ingredients. In a heat-proof bowl that will fit in the Instant Pot®, beat the sugar and butter with a hand mixer until the sugar has mostly dissolved and the mixture is light colored and fluffy. Add the egg yolks and beat until combined. Add the lemon zest, lemon juice, and salt and beat to combine. The mix-ture will probably appear grainy, but that's okay. Cover the bowl with aluminum foil.

2. Pressure cook the curd. Pour the water into the Instant Pot®. Place a trivet with handles in the pot and place the bowl on top. If your trivet doesn't have handles, use a foil sling (see page 16) to make removing the bowl easier. Lock the lid into place. Select Manual; adjust the pressure to High and the time to 10 minutes. After cooking, naturally release the pressure for 10 minutes, then quick release any remaining pressure. Unlock and remove the lid. Carefully remove the bowl from the pot and remove the foil. The mixture will appear clumpy and curdled.

3. Finish the curd. Whisk the curd mixture until it is smooth. Place a fine-mesh strainer over a medium bowl and pour the curd through it, pressing it down with a flexible spatula to pass the curd through, leaving the zest and any curdled egg bits behind. Be sure to scrape any curd on the outside bottom of the strainer into the bowl. Cover with plastic wrap, pushing the wrap down on top of the curd to keep a skin from forming. Refrigerate until set, 2 to 4 hours. The curd can be refrigerated for several days or frozen for up to a month in an airtight container.

SERVING TIP: Lemon curd makes a delicious addition to Cheesecake (page 211) or Yogurt (page 230). It's also wonderful mixed with whipped cream to make a simple lemon mousse, or as a topping for pound cake or shortbread.

PER SERVING (2 TABLESPOONS) Calories: 101; Fat: 5g; Sodium: 43mg; Carbohydrates: 13g; Fiber: 0g; Protein: 1g

ARRABBIATA SAUCE

This mildly spicy tomato sauce is a very useful kitchen staple to have on hand. It comes together quickly and keeps for a week or so in the refrigerator or for a month in the freezer. It's delicious on pizza or as a sauce with Vegetarian Lasagna (page 111) or spaghetti, either alone or with meat added. **MAKES 4 CUPS**

PREP AND FINISHING
20 minutes

MANUAL
12 minutes
high pressure

RELEASE
Natural for 10 minutes

**TOTAL TIME
40 MINUTES**

60 MIN OR LESS

GRAIN-FREE

DAIRY-FREE

3 tablespoons extra-virgin olive oil

1 small onion, minced

4 garlic cloves, minced

2 tablespoons minced or puréed sun-dried tomatoes

1 (28-ounce) can crushed tomatoes

½ teaspoon kosher salt, plus more to taste

1 teaspoon red pepper flakes, divided

¼ cup chopped fresh parsley

1. Start the sauce. Preheat the Instant Pot® by selecting Sauté and adjust to More for high heat. Heat the oil until it shimmers. Add the onion and garlic and cook, stirring frequently, until the vegetables have started to soften, 2 to 3 minutes. Stir in the sun-dried tomatoes and cook until fragrant, about 1 minute. Pour in the crushed tomatoes and stir to combine, scraping the bottom of the pot to loosen any browned bits that may have stuck. Stir in the salt and ½ teaspoon of red pepper flakes.

2. Pressure cook the sauce. Lock the lid into place. Select Manual; adjust the pressure to High and the time to 12 minutes. After cooking, naturally release the pressure for 10 minutes, then quick release any remaining pressure. Unlock and remove the lid.

3. Finish the sauce. Let the sauce cool for about 10 minutes, then stir in the remaining ½ teaspoon of red pepper flakes and the parsley. Taste and adjust the seasoning, adding more salt if necessary. Refrigerate or freeze in an airtight container if not using right away.

PER SERVING (1 CUP) Calories: 187; Fat: 11g; Sodium: 676mg; Carbohydrates: 20g; Fiber: 7g; Protein: 5g

SMOKY BARBECUE SAUCE

I'm not a big fan of commercial barbecue sauces—I find them way too sweet for my taste. I prefer this one, with its undertone of ancho chile and the smoke it gets from the paprika and chipotle. It's a bit spicy, but it has a good balance of acid and sugar. Use it for Barbecued Beef Sandwiches (page 187), or brushed on chicken or ribs before broiling or grilling. **MAKES 2 CUPS**

PREP AND FINISHING
10 minutes

MANUAL
8 minutes
high pressure

RELEASE
Natural for 5 minutes

**TOTAL TIME
30 MINUTES**

30 MIN OR LESS

GRAIN-FREE

1 dried ancho chile

1 small onion, cut into eighths

2 garlic cloves, lightly smashed

1½ cups strained tomatoes or tomato sauce

2 tablespoons unsalted butter

1 tablespoon apple cider vinegar

1 tablespoon molasses

1 teaspoon chipotle purée (see page 22)

1 teaspoon Worcestershire sauce

2 tablespoons brown sugar

1 teaspoon smoked paprika

1 teaspoon mustard powder

1 teaspoon kosher salt

½ teaspoon freshly ground black pepper

1. Prepare the chile. Pull or cut off the stem from the chile and remove as many seeds as possible. Put the chile in the Instant Pot®. Be sure to thoroughly wash your hands after handling the chile.

2. Pressure cook. Add the onion, garlic, strained tomatoes, butter, vinegar, molasses, chipotle purée, Worcestershire sauce, brown sugar, paprika, mustard powder, salt, and black pepper to the Instant Pot®. Lock the lid into place. Select Manual; adjust the pressure to High and the time to 8 minutes. After cooking, naturally release the pressure for 5 minutes, then quick release any remaining pressure. Unlock and remove the lid.

3. Finish the sauce. Pour the sauce into a blender. Blend until smooth, being careful to hold the lid on. Use immediately, or store in a covered container in the refrigerator for up to a week or in the freezer for up to a month.

PER SERVING (2 TABLESPOONS) Calories: 32; Fat: 2g; Sodium: 283mg; Carbohydrates: 4g; Fiber: 1g; Protein: 1g

ANCHO CHILE SAUCE

Of all the sauces I make, this is definitely in the top three for both flavor and utility. Not only does it make delicious Red Chicken Enchiladas (page 151), but it's a perfect base for Chili con Carne (page 190), and it adds a delightful piquancy to most Mexican or southwestern dishes. **MAKES 2 CUPS**

PREP AND FINISHING
10 minutes

MANUAL
8 minutes
high pressure

RELEASE
Natural for 5 minutes

TOTAL TIME
30 MINUTES

30 MIN OR LESS

GRAIN-FREE

DAIRY-FREE

2 ounces dried ancho chiles (3 to 5 chiles)

2 garlic cloves, lightly smashed

1½ cups water

2 teaspoons kosher salt

1½ teaspoons sugar

½ teaspoon dried oregano

½ teaspoon ground cumin

2 tablespoons apple cider vinegar

1. Prepare the chiles. Pull or cut off the stems from the chiles and remove as many seeds as possible. Put the chiles in the Instant Pot®. Be sure to thoroughly wash your hands after handling the chiles.

2. Pressure cook. Add the garlic, water, salt, sugar, oregano, and cumin to the Instant Pot®. Lock the lid into place. Select Manual; adjust the pressure to High and the time to 8 minutes. After cooking, naturally release the pressure for 5 minutes, then quick release any remaining pressure. Unlock and remove the lid.

3. Finish the sauce. Pour the sauce into a blender. Add the vinegar and blend until smooth, being careful to hold the lid on. Use immediately, or store in a covered container in the refrigerator for up to a week or in the freezer for up to a month.

INGREDIENT TIP: For a deeper flavor, toast the chiles after removing the stems and seeds. You can do this in a skillet over medium-high heat for about 30 seconds per side, or in a preheated 350°F oven for 5 to 7 minutes, just until the chiles are fragrant. Then put them in the Instant Pot® and proceed with step 2 of this recipe.

PER SERVING (2 TABLESPOONS) Calories: 4; Fat: 0g; Sodium: 305mg; Carbohydrates: 1g; Fiber: 0g; Protein: 0g

HOT PEPPER SAUCE

And now for something completely different—making your own hot pepper sauce. Think Tabasco or Crystal brands, but it's your very own blend. It's easy, but it does require care. Always remember that the capsaicin in chiles is very volatile and will burn your throat and nasal passages if you breathe it in. So don't quick release any steam at all once the sauce is cooked, and also be careful after blending the sauce. Don't use an immersion blender, as that can splash and aerosolize the capsaicin. **MAKES ABOUT 2 CUPS**

PREP AND FINISHING
15 minutes

MANUAL
1 minute
high pressure

RELEASE
Natural

**TOTAL TIME
20 MINUTES**

60 MIN OR LESS

GRAIN-FREE

DAIRY-FREE

12 ounces fresh hot chiles, such as serrano, jalapeño, or Fresno

1 dried chipotle chile or 2 teaspoons chipotle purée (see page 22)

1¼ cups apple cider vinegar, plus more as needed

1 teaspoon kosher salt

1. Prepare the chiles. Remove the stems from the fresh chiles and quarter them. Remove the stem from the dried chipotle (if using). Put the chiles in the Instant Pot®. Be sure to thoroughly wash your hands after handling the chiles.

2. Pressure cook. Add the vinegar and salt to the Instant Pot®. If the chiles are not submerged in vinegar, add more (or use water for a less intense sauce) just to cover. Lock the lid into place. Select Manual; adjust the pressure to High and the time to 1 minute. After cooking, naturally release the pressure until the pin has dropped. Wait another 5 minutes, then unlock the lid. Very carefully lift the lid so the steam is directed away from you.

3. Finish the sauce. Carefully pour the liquid and chiles into a blender. Blend until puréed. Carefully remove the lid; avoid breathing in the fumes coming from the blender. Strain the sauce through a coarse sieve into a glass container with a tight-fitting lid. The hot sauce will keep in the refrigerator almost indefinitely.

PER SERVING (2 TABLESPOONS) Calories: 11; Fat: 0g; Sodium: 233mg; Carbohydrates: 2g; Fiber: 0g; Protein: 0g

CHOCOLATE-CARAMEL SAUCE

Anyone who's made caramel the old-fashioned way on the stove knows that it requires constant attention—stirring at the right time, not stirring at the wrong time so it doesn't crystalize, and avoiding a boil-over when the cream goes in. No more of that for me now that I've discovered caramel sauce in the pressure cooker. This recipe yields a silky-smooth, perfectly balanced chocolate-caramel sauce that's outstanding as a topping for ice cream or Cheesecake (page 211), or as a spread for sandwich cookies. **MAKES ABOUT 2 CUPS**

PREP AND FINISHING
20 minutes

MANUAL
50 minutes
high pressure

RELEASE
Natural for 30 minutes

TOTAL TIME
1 HOUR 45 MINUTES

GRAIN-FREE

1 (14-ounce) can sweetened condensed milk

¼ cup heavy (whipping) cream

1 tablespoon unsalted butter, at room temperature

½ teaspoon vanilla extract

¼ teaspoon kosher salt

3 ounces bittersweet chocolate, chopped

1. Pressure cook. Pour the condensed milk into a heat-proof 2-cup measuring cup or small bowl that is large enough to fit all the ingredients. Cover the cup with aluminum foil and crimp the edges over the top. Place the cup in the Instant Pot® and add enough water to the pot to reach the level of the milk in the cup. Lock the lid into place. Select Manual; adjust the pressure to High and the time to 50 minutes. After cooking, naturally release the pressure for 20 minutes, then quick release any remaining pressure. Unlock and remove the lid.

2. Finish the sauce. Lift the cup out of the pot and remove the foil. Add the cream, butter, vanilla, and salt. Use an immersion blender to blend the sauce until it's smooth. While the sauce is still hot, add the chocolate and whisk to melt it into the caramel. Use right away, or refrigerate in an airtight container for several weeks.

INGREDIENT TIP: For plain caramel sauce, simply omit the chocolate. For salted caramel sauce, add ½ teaspoon more of kosher salt.

PER SERVING (2 TABLESPOONS) Calories: 121; Fat: 5g; Sodium: 76mg; Carbohydrates: 17g; Fiber: 0g; Protein: 2g

INSTANT POT® PRESSURE COOKING TIME CHARTS

The following charts provide approximate times for a variety of foods. To begin, you may want to cook for a minute or two less than the times listed; you can always simmer foods at natural pressure to finish cooking.

Keep in mind that these times are for the foods partially submerged in water (or broth) or steamed, and for the foods cooked alone. The cooking times for the same foods when they are part of a recipe may differ because of additional ingredients or cooking liquids, or a different release method than the one listed here.

For any foods labeled with "natural" release, allow at least 15 minutes natural pressure release before quick releasing any remaining pressure.

BEANS AND LEGUMES

When cooking beans, if you have 1 pound or more, it's best to use low pressure and increase the cooking time by a minute or two (with larger amounts, there's more chance for foaming at high pressure). If you have less than 1 pound, high pressure is fine. A little oil in the cooking liquid will reduce foaming. Unless a shorter release time is indicated, let the beans release naturally for at least 15 minutes, after which any remaining pressure can be quick released.

	MINUTES UNDER PRESSURE **UNSOAKED**	MINUTES UNDER PRESSURE **SOAKED IN SALTED WATER**	PRESSURE	RELEASE
BLACK BEANS	22 25	10 12	High Low	Natural
BLACK-EYED PEAS	12 15	5 7	High Low	Natural for 8 minutes, then quick
CANNELLINI BEANS	25 28	8 10	High Low	Natural
CHICKPEAS (GARBANZO BEANS)	18 20	3 4	High Low	Natural for 3 minutes, then quick
KIDNEY BEANS	25 28	8 10	High Low	Natural
LENTILS	10	not recommended	High	Quick
NAVY BEANS	18 20	8 10	High Low	Natural
PINTO BEANS	25 28	10 12	High Low	Natural
SPLIT PEAS (UNSOAKED)	5 (firm peas) to 8 (soft peas)	not recommended	High	Natural
LIMA BEANS	15 18	4 5	High Low	Natural for 5 minutes, then quick
SOY BEANS, FRESH (EDAMAME)	1	not recommended	High	Quick
SOYBEANS, DRIED	25 28	12 14	High Low	Natural

GRAINS

To prevent foaming, it's best to rinse these grains thoroughly before cooking, or include a small amount of butter or oil with the cooking liquid. Unless a shorter release time is indicated, let the grains release naturally for at least 15 minutes, after which any remaining pressure can be quick released.

	LIQUID PER 1 CUP OF GRAIN	MINUTES UNDER PRESSURE	PRESSURE	RELEASE
ARBORIO (OR OTHER MEDIUM-GRAIN) RICE	1½ cups	6	High	Quick
BARLEY, PEARLED	2½ cups	10	High	Natural
BROWN RICE, MEDIUM GRAIN	1⅓ cups	6–8	High	Natural
BROWN RICE, LONG GRAIN	1½ cups	13	High	Natural for 10 minutes, then quick
BUCKWHEAT	1¾ cups	2–4	High	Natural
FARRO, WHOLE GRAIN	3 cups	22–24	High	Natural
FARRO, PEARLED	2 cups	6–8	High	Natural
OATS, ROLLED	3 cups	3–4	High	Quick
OATS, STEEL CUT	4 cups	12	High	Natural
QUINOA	2 cups	2	High	Quick
WHEAT BERRIES	2 cups	30	High	Natural for 10 minutes, then quick
WHITE RICE, LONG GRAIN	1½ cups	3	High	Quick
WILD RICE	2½ cups	18–20	High	Natural

MEAT

Except as noted, these times are for braised meats—that is, meats that are seared before pressure cooking and partially submerged in liquid. Unless a shorter release time is indicated, let the meat release naturally for at least 15 minutes, after which any remaining pressure can be quick released.

	MINUTES UNDER PRESSURE	PRESSURE	RELEASE
BEEF, SHOULDER (CHUCK) ROAST (2 LB.)	35	High	Natural
BEEF, SHOULDER (CHUCK), 2" CHUNKS	20	High	Natural for 10 minutes
BEEF, BONE-IN SHORT RIBS	40	High	Natural
BEEF, FLAT IRON STEAK, CUT INTO ½" STRIPS	1	Low	Quick
BEEF, SIRLOIN STEAK, CUT INTO ½" STRIPS	1	Low	Quick
LAMB, SHOULDER, 2" CHUNKS	35	High	Natural
LAMB, SHANKS	40	High	Natural
PORK, SHOULDER ROAST (2 LB.)	25	High	Natural
PORK, SHOULDER, 2" CHUNKS	20	High	Natural
PORK, TENDERLOIN	4	Low	Quick
PORK, BACK RIBS (STEAMED)	30	High	Quick
PORK, SPARE RIBS (STEAMED)	20	High	Quick
PORK, SMOKED SAUSAGE, ½" SLICES	20	High	Quick

POULTRY

Except as noted, these times are for braised poultry—that is, partially submerged in liquid. Unless a shorter release time is indicated, let the poultry release naturally for at least 15 minutes, after which any remaining pressure can be quick released.

	MINUTES UNDER PRESSURE	PRESSURE	RELEASE
CHICKEN BREAST, BONE-IN (STEAMED)	8	Low	Natural for 5 minutes
CHICKEN BREAST, BONELESS (STEAMED)	5	Low	Natural for 8 minutes
CHICKEN THIGH, BONE-IN	15	High	Natural for 10 minutes
CHICKEN THIGH, BONELESS	8	High	Natural for 10 minutes
CHICKEN THIGH, BONELESS, 1"–2" PIECES	5	High	Quick
CHICKEN, WHOLE (SEARED ON ALL SIDES)	12–14	Low	Natural for 8 minutes
DUCK QUARTERS, BONE-IN	35	High	Quick
TURKEY BREAST, TENDERLOIN (12 OZ.) (STEAMED)	5	Low	Natural for 8 minutes
TURKEY THIGH, BONE-IN	30	High	Natural

FISH AND SEAFOOD

All times are for steamed fish and shellfish.

	MINUTES UNDER PRESSURE	PRESSURE	RELEASE
CLAMS	2	High	Quick
MUSSELS	1	High	Quick
SALMON, FRESH (1" THICK)	5	Low	Quick
HALIBUT, FRESH (1" THICK)	3	High	Quick
TILAPIA OR COD, FRESH	1	Low	Quick
TILAPIA OR COD, FROZEN	3	Low	Quick
LARGE SHRIMP, FROZEN	1	Low	Quick

VEGETABLES

The cooking method for all the following vegetables is steaming; if the vegetables are cooked in liquid, the times may vary. Green vegetables will be tender-crisp; root vegetables will be soft. Unless a shorter release time is indicated, let the vegetables release naturally for at least 15 minutes, after which any remaining pressure can be quick released.

	PREP	MINUTES UNDER PRESSURE	PRESSURE	RELEASE
ACORN SQUASH	Halved	9	High	Quick
ARTICHOKES, LARGE	Whole	15	High	Quick
BEETS	Quartered if large; halved if small	9	High	Natural
BROCCOLI	Cut into florets	1	Low	Quick
BRUSSELS SPROUTS	Halved	2	High	Quick
BUTTERNUT SQUASH	Peeled, ½" chunks	8	High	Quick
CABBAGE	Sliced	5	High	Quick
CARROTS	½"–1" slices	2	High	Quick
CAULIFLOWER	Whole	6	High	Quick
CAULIFLOWER	Cut into florets	1	Low	Quick
GREEN BEANS	Cut in halves or thirds	1	Low	Quick
POTATOES, LARGE RUSSET (FOR MASHING)	Quartered	8	High	Natural for 8 minutes
POTATOES, RED	Whole if less than 1½" across, halved if larger	4	High	Quick
SPAGHETTI SQUASH	Halved lengthwise	7	High	Quick
SWEET POTATOES	Halved lengthwise	8	High	Natural

MEASUREMENT CONVERSIONS

VOLUME EQUIVALENTS (LIQUID)

US STANDARD	US STANDARD (OUNCES)	METRIC (APPROXIMATE)
2 tablespoons	1 fl. oz.	30 mL
¼ cup	2 fl. oz.	60 mL
½ cup	4 fl. oz.	120 mL
1 cup	8 fl. oz.	240 mL
1½ cups	12 fl. oz.	355 mL
2 cups or 1 pint	16 fl. oz.	475 mL
4 cups or 1 quart	32 fl. oz.	1 L
1 gallon	128 fl. oz.	4 L

OVEN TEMPERATURES

FAHRENHEIT (F)	CELSIUS (C) (APPROXIMATE)
250°	120°
300°	150°
325°	165°
350°	180°
375°	190°
400°	200°
425°	220°
450°	230°

VOLUME EQUIVALENTS (DRY)

US STANDARD	METRIC (APPROXIMATE)
⅛ teaspoon	0.5 mL
¼ teaspoon	1 mL
½ teaspoon	2 mL
¾ teaspoon	4 mL
1 teaspoon	5 mL
1 tablespoon	15 mL
¼ cup	59 mL
⅓ cup	79 mL
½ cup	118 mL
⅔ cup	156 mL
¾ cup	177 mL
1 cup	235 mL
2 cups or 1 pint	475 mL
3 cups	700 mL
4 cups or 1 quart	1 L

WEIGHT EQUIVALENTS

US STANDARD	METRIC (APPROXIMATE)
½ ounce	15 g
1 ounce	30 g
2 ounces	60 g
4 ounces	115 g
8 ounces	225 g
12 ounces	340 g
16 ounces or 1 pound	455 g

THE DIRTY DOZEN & THE CLEAN FIFTEEN

A nonprofit environmental watchdog organization called Environmental Working Group (EWG) looks at data supplied by the US Department of Agriculture (USDA) and the Food and Drug Administration (FDA) about pesticide residues. Each year it compiles lists of the highest and lowest pesticide loads found in commercial crops. You can use these lists to decide which fruits and vegetables to buy organic to minimize your exposure to pesticides and which produce is considered safe enough to buy conventionally. This does not mean they are pesticide-free, though, so wash these fruits and vegetables thoroughly.

DIRTY DOZEN

Apples
Celery
Cherries
Cherry tomatoes
Cucumbers
Grapes

Nectarines
Peaches
Spinach
Strawberries
Sweet bell peppers
Tomatoes

In addition to the Dirty Dozen, the EWG added two types of produce contaminated with highly toxic organo-phosphate insecticides:

Kale/collard greens   Hot peppers

CLEAN FIFTEEN

Asparagus
Avocados
Cabbage
Cantaloupe
Cauliflower
Eggplant
Grapefruit
Honeydew melon

Kiwi
Mangos
Onions
Papayas
Pineapples
Sweet corn
Sweet peas (frozen)

RECIPE INDEX

	30 MIN OR LESS	60 MIN OR LESS	ONE POT	GRAIN-FREE	DAIRY-FREE
Almond-Date Oatmeal, 41–42		X	X		
Almond-Parmesan Pilaf, 92–93	X				
Ancho Chile Sauce, 239	X			X	X
Arrabbiata Sauce, 237		X		X	X
Asparagus Ends Soup, 50–51		X		X	
Baked Potato Soup, 104–105		X	X		
Balsamic and Honey–Glazed Chicken and Carrots, 142–143		X		X	X
Barbecued Beef Sandwiches, 187		X	X		X
Barley Salad with Red Cabbage and Feta, 95		X	X		
Beef Vindaloo, 201		X	X		X
Better Than Mom's Potato Salad, 72–73	X			X	
Black-Eyed Peas and Greens, 84–85			X	X	X
Black Pepper and Parmesan Corn on the Cob, 52–53	X				
Braised Green Beans with Bacon, 69	X			X	X
Brazilian Chicken Thighs with Dark Beer, 168–169		X			X
Broccoli and Cauliflower with Cheese Sauce, 64	X				
Brown and Wild Rice Stuffed Peppers, 98–99		X			
Browned-Butter Apple Spice Cake, 220–221		X			
Butternut Squash Risotto, 108–109		X	X		
Cajun Creamed Corn, 54	X		X		
Cajun-Spiced Turkey Breast, 164–165		X	X		
Caprese Risotto, 108–109		X	X		
Caramelized Banana Pudding, 208–209				X	
Carnitas, 176–177		X		X	X

	30 MIN OR LESS	60 MIN OR LESS	ONE POT	GRAIN-FREE	DAIRY-FREE
Hot Pepper Sauce, 240		X		X	X
Hummus with Avocado, 82–83				X	X
Individual Spinach Quiches in Ham Cups, 43	X			X	
Irish Cream Cheesecake, 211–213					
Italian Chickpea Stew with Pesto, 87–88				X	
Italian Pot Roast, 194–195				X	X
Italian-Style Lamb Shanks with White Beans, 199–200			X	X	X
Lemon-Blueberry Cheesecake, 211–213					
Lemon Curd, 234–235				X	
Lemon-Gingersnap Parfaits, 219		X			
Lemon Yogurt, 230–232				X	
Lentils with Short Ribs, 90–91			X	X	X
Maple Sausage Breakfast Casserole, 38–39		X	X		
Marbled–Cream Cheese Pumpkin Pie, 214–215					
Margarita Pie, 224–225					
Mashed Sweet Potatoes with Toasted Almonds, 57–58		X		X	
Mexican-American-Style Enchiladas, 151–152		X			
Milk-Braised Chicken with Lemon-Garlic Sauce, 148–149		X		X	
Mulligatawny Soup, 138–139		X	X		
Mushroom-Pea Risotto, 108–109		X	X		
Mussels with Red Pepper–Garlic Sauce, 129	X		X	X	
New York Cheesecake, 211–213					
Nutella-Banana Oatmeal, 41–42		X	X		
Orange Chicken, 146–147		X	X		X
Parmesan Turkey Meatballs, 161–162	X		X		
Peas and Parsley Pilaf, 92–93	X				
Peel-and-Eat Shrimp, 122–123	X		X	X	
Peel-and-Eat Shrimp with Cocktail Sauce, 122–123	X		X	X	
Peel-and-Eat Shrimp with Remoulade, 122–123	X		X	X	

	30 MIN OR LESS	60 MIN OR LESS	ONE POT	GRAIN-FREE	DAIRY-FREE
Penne Bolognese, 202–203		X	X		
Penne Caponata, 114–115	X		X		
Perfect Chicken Breast, 140–141	X		X	X	
Perfect Chicken Breast with Coconut-Curry Sauce, 140–141	X		X	X	
Perfect Chicken Breast with Creamy Pesto Sauce, 140–141	X		X	X	
Perfect Chicken Breast with Romesco Sauce, 140–141	X		X	X	
Pickled Beets, 70–71				X	X
Poached Eggs, 36–37	X			X	X
Poached Salmon with Mustard Cream Sauce, 131	X		X	X	
Polenta, 97		X			
Pork Loin Braised in Milk, 180–181		X		X	
Pork Shoulder, 185–186		X	X		X
Pork Shoulder with Cajun Sauce, 185–186		X	X		X
Pork Shoulder with Ginger-Soy Sauce, 185–186		X	X		X
Pork Shoulder with Jerk Sauce, 185–186		X	X		X
Pork Tenderloin with Cabbage and Noodles, 178–179	X		X		X
Quick Beef Stew, 192–193		X	X		X
Quinoa and Corn Soup, 65	X		X		X
Quinoa Salad with Beets and Sweet Potatoes, 96		X	X		X
Raspberry-Peach Yogurt, 230–232				X	
Red Chicken Enchiladas, 151–152		X			
Red Pepper and Tomato Bisque with Parmesan Croutons, 102–103		X			
Red Wine–Braised Short Ribs, 188–189			X	X	X
Refried Black Beans, 80–81				X	X
Rice Pilaf, 92–93	X				
Risotto, 108–109		X	X		
Sesame-Soy Chicken Wings, 153	X		X		X
Smoky Barbecue Sauce, 238	X			X	
Smoky Black Bean Tacos, 116–117			X		
Smoky-Sweet Spare Ribs, 175		X			X

INDEX

ACKNOWLEDGMENTS

I'd like to thank the members and moderators of the discussion forums of eGullet.org and the Facebook Instant Pot®® Community group, who made it easy to immerse myself in all things Instant Pot®. And thanks to Stacy Wagner-Kinnear and the great editorial and design team at Callisto Media for all their work on the book.

ABOUT THE AUTHOR

JANET A. ZIMMERMAN is the author of *The Healthy Pressure Cooker Cookbook*. A longtime pressure cooking enthusiast, she was quickly won over by the ease and convenience of the Instant Pot®. For more than 15 years Janet has shared her love of cooking with others as a food writer and culinary instructor. Today she writes, teaches, and pressure cooks in Atlanta, Georgia.

CPSIA information can be obtained
at www.ICGtesting.com
Printed in the USA
BVOW05s1202120617

486515BV00001BA/1/P

31901060923416